Vulnerable Embrace

Sermons as Worship

Rev. Elana Keppel Levy
Rev. Lucus Levy Keppel

Parson's Porch Books
www.parsonsporchbooks.com

Vulnerable Embrace: Sermons as Worship
ISBN: Softcover 978-1-949888-13-3
Copyright © 2018 by Elana Keppel Levy *&* Lucus Levy Keppel

All rights reserved. No part of this book may be reproduced or transmitted in any form or by any means, electronic or mechanical, including photocopying, recording, or by any information storage and retrieval system, without permission in writing from the publisher.

Vulnerable Embrace

Rev. Elana Levy and Rev. Lucus Keppel have been serving as co-pastors of Trinity Presbyterian Church in Bixby, Oklahoma since 2016. This is their first call together as a clergy couple.

REV. ELANA KEPPEL LEVY

Rev. Elana Levy sees God's work inscribed throughout the world. Growing up with a Jewish father and Presbyterian mother, religious conversations were all playful and interfaith. Engaging and appreciating difference meant that exact agreement was not required to cultivate a beautiful life that pleases God.

From a very young age, Elana has been drawn to the study of the Holocaust, particularly those who acted with such cruelty. She learned German in school and received undergraduate degrees in German language and psychology. She spent ten years translating documents about concentration camp guards. She pursues questions: How could humans do this? Who are we when we stray from our creaturely calling? What can Christians do to cultivate justice? These unanswerable questions prompt her to see people as people first and to reach out even when hope seems lost.

After college, Elana earned a Masters of Social Work with a special focus on older adults, the bereaved, and those traumatized by sexual assault. God's presence is most strongly felt when we are present, attentive, and loving to one another. Feeling strongly called to the ministry, Elana completed her Masters of Divinity and received a call as a Pastoral Care Associate in Roswell, NM (where she ministered to all comers, even aliens!). Elana loves movies (and quoting them!); games and puzzles; deep conversations that come out of nowhere; prayer from the heart; and moments of genuine human kindness. She can't wait to welcome you in to sit and visit for a spell.

REV. LUCUS LEVY KEPPEL

An ordained Presbyterian Pastor since 2013, Lucus received a Masters of Divinity from Louisville Seminary in 2012 and holds a Master of Arts in Electronic Media Management from Central Michigan University. Prior to his ministry at Trinity Presbyterian Church in Bixby, OK, Lucus served two churches together in central New Mexico; hosted the Morning Show at the Catholic radio station KNOM in Nome, Alaska; and worked with the Night Ministry, offering food and fellowship to people experiencing homelessness on the streets of Chicago, IL.

When he's not at work, Lucus enjoys playing board games and role-playing games, acting in community theatre productions, filming and editing short videos, and reading science fiction/fantasy novels.

In his preaching, Lucus seeks to bring Scripture to life through storytelling, history, and theatre. He loves to make connections between the historical context of the scriptures and our present-day circumstances, especially as they relate to seeing God's love in the world. That divine love calls everyone to work together for peace, justice, and understanding – so let's get to work!

Contents

Foreword 11

Acknowledgements 13

Introduction 17

There is Still a Vision (Rev. Elana Levy) 23

What is God Like? (Rev. Lucus Keppel) 27

Anger or Righteousness? (Rev. Elana Levy) 35

Testing God (Revs. Levy & Keppel) 39

Love Will Seek You (Rev. Elana Levy) 45

Refining the Soul (Rev. Lucus Keppel) 48

Alive in Christ Jesus (Rev. Elana Levy) 53

Campfire (Rev. Lucus Keppel) 59

Truth, Not Tricks (Rev. Elana Levy) 65

Voice at the Gate (Rev. Lucus Keppel) 69

A Vulnerable Embrace (Rev. Elana Levy) 77

The God Who Gave You Birth (Rev. Elana Levy) 80

The Joy of… Work?! (Rev. Elana Levy) 87

Mary Speaks and Bartholomew Speaks (Revs. Levy & Keppel) ... 91

Soul Debt (Rev. Lucus Keppel) 98

Is This Love? (Rev. Elana Levy) 105

If You Had Been Here (Rev. Elana Levy) 110

Being the Beloved Child (Rev. Lucus Keppel) 117

Hlāfweard (Rev. Elana Levy) 122

I AM the Network (Rev. Lucus Keppel) 127

Out-of-this-World Communion (Rev. Lucus Keppel) 131

Agape (Rev. Lucus Keppel) 137

Called to Freedom (Rev. Elana Levy) 143

Connecting with the Spirit (Rev. Lucus Keppel) 147

The Treasure of Dunkin' John (Rev. Lucus Keppel) 151

Homelight (Rev. Lucus Keppel) 155

Index… 160

Foreword
(Rev. Deborah Fortel and Rev. Dr. David Sawyer)

Churches are facing many significant challenges and recognizing the need for transformation in response to the constantly increasing pace of change. We all have our suggestions of what the church needs right now, but this book is an example of one thing the church needs: to listen to the voices of its young leaders. Elana and Lucus are pastors in their first decade of congregational ministry. Their collection of sermons gives us a glimpse at the basics for "new church," "next church," and "fresh expressions."

These sermons reflect the unique backgrounds, academic training, and non-church work experience of Elana and Lucus. They fold careful Biblical research, and relevant theological reflection into a mix of popular culture and current events to meet the spiritual and emotional needs of their congregation. Even their word-studies are charming. In other words, these are really engaging, attractive, witty people who preach thought-provoking and helpful sermons.

We first met them when they were students at Louisville Presbyterian Seminary. David remembers their imaginative contributions to the weekly meetings of the innovative student worship design team. Deborah remembers Lucus' early sermons and the helpful insights he brought to his colleagues in a small preaching group. We were excited to be part of Lucus' ordination service in his home church in Michigan. We have followed their paths in ministry with great affection.

We have relished these sermons with illustrations from chemistry to scout craft, from cell phone networks to the St. Joseph lighthouse on Lake Michigan; from hard images like domestic violence to sweet comparisons of prayer types as "dozing kitten prayers" versus "yapping dog prayers." Go ahead, reader, and learn, as we have, from these preachers.

We said the church needs to listen to the voices of its younger members. But there is more to be said. When middle-aged and Boomer generation church leaders worry about how to manage their own leadership and still involve younger leaders, we offer what has worked for us. As older, more experienced leaders, we know we still have something to offer in providing the perspectives of history, accumulated wisdom, and encouragement to those who are younger than we. But it is time to step back and pass the baton to this generation. Elana and Lucus may not preach and lead the way we would.

And that's how it should be. That's what the church needs right now. We say to our cohort: "Let our young leaders lead!"

Deborah Fortel and David Sawyer of Flourishing Church Consulting and Coaching have been pastors, interim pastors, denominational administrators, and college and seminary teachers. They are authors, most recently, of *Pathmarks to New Church: A Workbook for Leaders of Communities in Search of Innovation.*

Acknowledgements

Elana Keppel Levy – I often tell people that pastoral work is like building sandcastles. We dedicate so much care and attention to being with people, crafting liturgy, studying scripture, searching for the Spirit and working to translate that into a sermon that people can really hear. Then, when the day is past – maybe something remains or maybe the seas and the winds wash it away to be rebuilt day by day. What this metaphor fails to capture, though, is that it is not possible to walk in faith alone. We are all formed and reforming, shaped by those who came before us just as we help one another to find new designs to inhabit. For all those builders, designers, engineers, water watchers, and artists, I give thanks.

For their constant love and playful curiosity, I thank my parents, Fred and Cindy Levy. Being of two different faiths, they decided not to put them in competition with one another. Rather, they presented the best of what they believed and encouraged my brother and I to follow our own paths. Being of two different personalities, they opened up worlds of possibility for me: to be the kite or the string, to be the one out front or the one behind the scenes, to engage beauty and fear with firm faith. I also thank my brother, Josh, for his fascinating breadth of historical knowledge – told in stories obscure, hilarious, and riveting. Even from a young age, he taught me the importance of knowing your stuff and having the confidence to stand by (and defend) what you assert.

There have been many pastors who have helped guide me along the way. Rev. Suzy Cothran over coffee (okay, of course I was having tea…) told me not to be a pastor if I could be anything else. That challenge never left me, and she may not even remember it. I once heard her preach when I was wandering from faith. She talked about seekers and gave me hope that even I might one day find. When I did find my way back to church it was at Faith Presbyterian in Greensboro, NC. Rev. Chris Tuttle was something of a revelation to me. He is thoughtful, caring, and intelligent. His sermons are powerful emotionally and spiritually, while still firmly rooted in academic rigor. He and the rest of Faith Presbyterian gave me a church home of my own. They opened their hearts to me and pushed me to engage more deeply. I didn't know I had anything to say until people like I.E. Martin wouldn't stop debating me and people like Betsy Rule started to tell me, "Say that again." It was at Faith Presbyterian that my "no, God, not me" became "yes, God, me!" Rev. John Johnson, the next pastor at Faith, dared me to preach a sermon, which I did – before I was even sure that pastoral ministry was my calling. For the encouragement that got me to be about as involved as an associate pastor (and opening up space for me to do so), I thank him.

Once I began the path to ordination and beyond, many people helped shore up my faltering places. Rev. Dr. Shannon Craigo-Snell – a woman of valor – transformed my theology, poured wisdom in my mind, and supported all my wild seminary endeavors. In many ways, she freed me up to be more faithful and she will always have my gratitude. Dr. Tyler Mayfield is as earnest and fearless an explorer of scripture as I have ever known. Rather than shying away from the difficult passages, the impossible theological problems, he deftly steers students towards them without abandoning us in our struggles. His humility and sincerity have meant more to me than he could know. It seems that I could write a novel about each of my professors, but I will cut short that impulse. Suffice it to say that Louisville Presbyterian Theological seminary was, for me, a place that was always striving to be a community, to hear all voices, to learn and grow together. May it continue to be so for many years to come.

I also want to thank the churches that helped bring me up as a baby pastor: Grace Immanuel UCC in Louisville, KY and First Presbyterian Church in Roswell, NM. Rev Dr. Greg Bain and Rev. Kent Leydens were more than mentors and teacher to me – you became my friends. For all the growing pains of ministry, I know they were eased by your care and attention. Thanks to both churches for helping me to learn and challenging me when I erred.

I want to thank Trinity Presbyterian Church in Bixby, Oklahoma and my silly beloved, Lucus. When I talk about this church, I can do nothing but boast – not because of anything that Lucus and I have done, but because of the love and grace that you all show day by day. Your openness to new ideas and your willingness to support us through difficult times are astounding and I thank God for the miracle of this place.

Finally, thank you for reading this book. We hope and pray that you find something to connect to – that the Spirit speaks to you and gives you the blessing and the strength that you need. May your sandcastle grow where it ought and be remade in God's love.

Lucus Levy Keppel – I appreciate greatly how much of my ministry has been shaped by the teachers and professors who either opened doors I didn't know had hinges, or who allowed me to push against them for long enough that I discovered what I truly believed. My thanks especially to Rev. Marjorie Wilhelmi and Rev. Anne Schaefer, who still teach through their love and acceptance, even of know-it-all kids like I was. And to Dr. Will Anderson, (senior member in good standing within Central Michigan University's regionally promoted school of broadcast and cinematic arts), thank you for helping me find my voice as a creator and leader, while, occasionally, overlooking my excessive use of commas – and dashes! Rev. Dr. Claudio Carvalhaes, I will never forget the time you donned the flying pig costume, and we danced around the quad at Louisville Seminary, celebrating the way the Holy Spirit interrupts and guides us in new ways. Rev. Dr. Amy Platinga Pauw, Rev. Dr. Shannon Craigo-Snell, and Rev. Dr. Chris Elwood all deserve much more praise than I can write in here, for their patience with me in Seminary while my theological world was turned upside down and returned with wider lenses.

The Rev. Dr. David Sawyer (who preached at my ordination) and the Rev. Deborah Fortel (who taught me to preach experientially) are also the first clergy couple I had met. Who knew that just a couple years after I graduated from Seminary, I'd be following in their footsteps with Elana?

There is so much to be grateful for from the congregations that helped form my faith. Those congregations include Jakarta Community Church (Jakarta, Indonesia), Orchard Lake Community Church (comma) Presbyterian (Orchard Lake, MI), Covenant Community Church (Louisville, KY), Ancho Community Presbyterian Church and Corona United Presbyterian Church (Collectively the Mountain Ministry Parish in the Presbytery of Sierra Blanca, NM). A special thanks to the Nome Ministerial Alliance (Nome, AK) for allowing me as a then not-yet-ordained Seminary graduate to participate in your council – and guest preach occasionally at your churches.

For our current call at Trinity Presbyterian Church in Bixby, OK – it means so much that you were willing to try the crazy idea of splitting a full-time call into two calls that Elana and I could fill together. We know that God has called us here and rejoice to serve God alongside of you.

To David Russell Tullock with Parson's Porch Book Company – how can we thank you enough for reaching out to us? It meant so much that you read our work and thought it worthy of printing.

Of course, I am always grateful to those who have been my life-long teachers in following Jesus' Way and navigating relationships: my parents, Ibu Beth and 'Pak Chuck. May you always have a lake on which to take the pontoon and find agreement.

Introduction

Rev. Neichelle Guidry Jones once wrote that good worship, "happens when we surrender and go with the flow of the Holy Spirit."[1] When you think about surrendering and going with the flow of the Spirit, a more or less strict order of worship is probably pretty far from your mind. Having a set, printed bulletin reflecting that predetermined order might seem like the last thing you'd want for spontaneous worship.

We honor and respect traditions of unprogrammed worship in their energy and vitality. Yet, there's something very special to us about having a bulletin during a worship service. It's your permanent guide to the impermanence of worship: the physical representation of the ephemeral, your touchstone to enter into the words of joy and sorrow of the whole body of Christ before being sent out to the world.

We had many choices about how to structure a book of sermons — chronological, following the liturgical calendar, by topic, and so on. We've chosen to structure it like a Reformed worship service, following the ancient rhythms of worship while always being reformed by the Word of God. First, we gather together as a local expression of the Body of Christ. In the call to worship, we're reminded that we are here to worship the Triune God – and that reminder leads us to sing praises to God. From there, it is natural to remember that we and the world are not as God intended - and are, in ourselves, unworthy to be in God's presence. Therefore, we confess our sin – and immediately receive an assurance of God's forgiveness. Filled with joy and humility in that forgiveness, we then pass the peace of Christ to one another.

After gathering together, the next part of the worship service is the Word of God proclaimed. By praying for the illumination of the Holy Spirit, singing praises to God, and reading the holy scriptures, we ask God to help us understand the Word revealed to us in Jesus Christ. In proclaiming the Word of God, we follow Jesus in lifting up the words of the Bible: "Love the Lord your God with all your heart, mind, soul, and strength, and love your neighbor as yourself."[2]

---

[1] Neichelle R. Guidry Jones, "Good Worship," *Liturgy* 29, no. 2 (2014):37.

[2] Luke 10:27

In response to the Word proclaimed, we affirm our faith, celebrate the sacraments of Baptism or Communion, as appropriate, to pledge our time and our treasure to the mission of the church, and pray for God's special attention for the Church and the world. All of these are responses to the Word – and "the proclamation of the Word is incomplete if it fails to evoke the response of the people of God."[3] Now, there's a challenge to the church!

Lastly, the congregation is charged with living a Christian life, taking what they have learned and felt in worship into their lives. In acts of commitment, through song and prayer, we go into the world in the love and service of God.

If you want to try out the ride of "order of worship" as order of sermons, climb aboard and read from cover to cover. However, the chapters in this book are independent of each other, written in most cases by one of us, but always very clearly marked with their inspiring scripture and author. So, feel free to jump around and read as the Spirit moves you. Sermons aren't for us, after all. First, they're for God and next they're for the hearers of the Word.

If you are curious about who we are and how this clergy couple thing works, then stick around. We're always happy to talk about our calling as a clergy couple, and other delightful, Spirit-filled oddities of our lives.

Being a clergy couple is kind of a foreign concept for many. Women were prevented from becoming pastors in the Presbyterian Church until the mid-late twentieth century, and even after being ordained, they usually weren't married to a fellow pastor. Even then, the number of pastors who are married to each other and serving the same church is a much smaller subset. Yet, the number of co-pastoring clergy couples is growing, within our denomination, the Presbyterian Church (USA). It's pretty clear to see why – many more couples are meeting in Seminary and falling in love with someone who shares their passion for pastoral work. And, now that same-sex marriage is legal, we are also at the very beginning of clergy couples that are not defined strictly by gender, too.

We have found working together as co-pastors to be wonderful. Each of us have strengths and areas of interest that differ from each other, and so, together, we are able to be more connected to the congregation we serve. We've shared the load of ministry, each about half-time in a single full-time position, and since both of us love to preach, we alternate just about every

---

[3] "Directory for Worship," in *Book of Order*, W-3.0301, Vol. 2. The Constitution of the Presbyterian Church (USA) (Louisville: Westminster Press, 2016), 89-90.

Sunday in the pulpit. Whoever's preaching that week gets to design the bulletin, choose hymns, write (or choose) liturgy, and of course, deliver the sermon. The other one acts in a sous-chef role, taking additional readings during the service and being the point person for pastoral calls that week.

Sometimes people ask us, "well, who's in charge? To this we respond, "first Jesus, then the Session"[4]. We believe that shared leadership is part of what it means to follow Christ. We are seldom content with a majority rules, winner-take-all dynamic of power. To us, the church should never be a place of winners and losers – a place where voices are drowned out and trampled on by those who can muster the stronger force. Jesus didn't bow to political pressure or powerful leaders. He went to the heart of what truly unites that and lifted it above all of our artificial boundaries and statuses and divisions. We worship God and serve neighbor – and we do it together without rank. What power we have in the church comes from God and belongs to God. It is never for us to insist on our own way or to harm the community inside and out. This is no small task and we could never even attempt it, but for the grace of God in Jesus Christ.

It is under that same grace that we offer you these sermons and this blessing: May you relax into the embrace of the Holy One, so that the heartbeat of God resounds through your being. May the Spirit of God breathe through these words that you may be inspired. And may the love of Jesus sustain you and buoy you up through storms of life. Amen.

~ Elana and Lucus, 2018

---

[4] For Presbyterians, the Session is the governing body of the local church, like a church board, council, or vestry.

Call to Worship

There is Still a Vision
(Rev. Elana Levy)
Psalm 33; Habakkuk 2:2-2:20

When we first meet Habakkuk, he is wrestling with the violence and injustice all around him – wrestling with his just God who wasn't preventing this evil. There's corruption and inequity and lawlessness in Judah's society, bearing down on the powerless. On top of that, the Chaldean (Babylonian) threat is looming larger and coming closer. The northern kingdom has already fallen. Would Judah, too, be conquered? Destroyed? Habakkuk was lost in the darkness, reaching out for God. In the second chapter of the book that bears his name, Habakkuk's prayer is answered. God speaks to him and to us to draw us out of the darkness. Here we remember that the shock of light that we can sometimes scarcely see steadily grows stronger and brighter – a flame coming into view and casting out shadows.

God says some powerful things to still Habakkuk's fear. First, God says, "Write the vision; make it plain on tablets, so that a runner may read it. For there is still a vision for the appointed time; it speaks of the end and does not lie." How do we challenge the overwhelming darkness? With a vision – a vision of light, of God's might, of the power of goodness. This vision calls us forward. If we have lost it, despair eats away at us. What we need to do is to claim a vision of God's glory – not a little one, just effective for a small moment in time, but a grand one, big enough for all time. We need a vision so large that someone running past can't help but see it in an instant. We need a vision that broadcasts to every city on earth because God spans mountains and oceans and continents and peoples. With a God so tremendous, a God of such brilliant light, how can we believe that darkness has the final say? How can we not begin with worship?

Here, God reminds us, the vision speaks, and it does not lie. So the question becomes: can we seek the Lord, wait for the Lord, trusting that the evil that gnaws at us will be answered by God Almighty? If goodness takes too long to break through, that does not mean that we give up. God says, "If [the vision] seems to tarry, wait for it; it will surely come, it will not delay." This could also be translated, "If the vision is delayed, long for it…" This vision of God overcoming is foundational to our faith and the deep yearning of our hearts follows from that faith. Keeping our hearts and minds focused on this vision fixes the hope and strength of trusting God deep within us.

And then we find a familiar line within God's speech – one that Paul picked up in the New Testament, "Look at the proud! Their spirit is not right in them, but the righteous live by their faith." This line is as simple as it is complex. On the surface, it seems straight forward: I know I don't want to be proud, so I'll live by my faith. Wonderful! Umm...faith in what, exactly?

The word here in Hebrew is 'emunah[5], which covers a lot of ground. The root of this word includes a verb that means enduring or caring for others, it is where we get the word "Amen" from, and it is the same root as the word that means "truth." Here, faith doesn't mean that we recited the right creed at the right time. 'emunah is a word that looks at our whole selves – our need to come to worship. The closest one-word translation would be, "the righteous live by faithfulness," but even that doesn't get the whole picture. This sense of faith includes mental and emotional steadfastness in depending on our Lord coupled with the actions that are inspired by that faith. The righteous do not live by abstract notions of faith; our trust in God inspires us to be conscientiousness and to perform acts of service. This is integrity motivated by a power far greater than our own will. Catching the vision and continuing to serve the cause of justice and goodness – that is how we live through the darkness, that is how we please God.

We remember dark and difficult times in our own history like the struggle for civil rights. We bring to mind the bold vision that Martin Luther King, Jr. held – a vision for a better life for all Americans regardless of their color or race or creed. He saw that violence, hatred, and prejudice tear down societies – that they do as much damage to the oppressed as they do to the oppressor. And he read the prophets and the Gospels – he saw God's promise that justice will roll down like water and righteousness like a mighty stream. He saw that God blessed a way of non-violence and patience and he offered himself up to the cause in every way possible. Rev. Dr. King lived this vision because what he saw from God meant more to him than those who doubted the possibility of a new way. It meant more to him than those who would come with vile words, with dogs and firehoses, with guns or with bombs.

As I reflected on this passage this week, I thought most about September 15, 1963. Birmingham, Alabama was well known as a dangerous place for those who pushed for civil rights. The atmosphere was tense, the city was segregated, and violence against black institutions happened regularly. The 16th Street Baptist Church became a rallying place for activists, starting a Children's Crusade and hosting civil rights leaders like Rev. Dr. King. They

---

[5] אמונה ('emunah)

spoke out, registered African Americans to vote; they worked for integration and change.

On the morning of Sunday September 15th, five children were in the basement of the church putting on choir robes, reading scripture, fixing their outfits. The sermon that morning was called, "A Love that Forgives." At least fifteen sticks of dynamite had been planted by members of the KKK. When they exploded, they blew a hole in the church's back wall that was seven feet across. Three of the girls that died in the explosion were 14 and the other was 11. About twenty others were injured. The bomb blew out all of the church's stained-glass windows except for one that showed Christ leading a group of young children.[6]

The scene was quickly flooded by about 2,000 African-Americans, hysterical and heartbroken. In an effort to bring calm, the pastor of the church recited Psalm 23 through a bullhorn. "The Lord is my shepherd…" This was truly a dark day, an unthinkable crime, a national tragedy. The mayor of Birmingham called the attack, "just sickening" and the FBI were called in to investigate. While white supremacists glorified the bombing, news of it spread nationally and internationally. People started to really see segregation and hatred bearing its rotten fruit. Many questioned whether they had done enough to move our country forward. An editorial in the Milwaukee Sentinel said, "For the rest of the nation, the Birmingham church bombing should serve to goad the conscience. The deaths…in a sense, are on the hands of each of us."[7]

Violence like this has no redeeming value. Evil run amok is a gruesome sight. And though the white supremacists may have thought they won the day, this incident along with the Birmingham campaign, the March on Washington, and the assassination of JFK moved the hearts and minds of Americans more and more. So much so that on July 2, 1964, President Lyndon Johnson signed the Civil Rights Act into law. Discrimination based on race, color, religion, gender, or national origin was now strictly against the law everywhere in this nation. The evil that the KKK dreamed up for that Sunday morning served to undermine their cause of hatred moving into the future.[8]

---

[6] "16th Street Baptist Church Bombing," *Wikipedia: The Free Encyclopedia*, Wikimedia Foundation Inc., updated 25 August 2018, https://en.wikipedia.org/wiki/16th_Street_Baptist_Church_bombing.

[7] Ibid

[8] Ibid

And this message rings loud and clear in Habakkuk: evil contains the seeds of its own undoing. Those who heap up material wealth for themselves will fall prey to their creditors. Those who loot and plunder from conquered peoples will face angry mobs returning violence with violence. Those who misuse others to gain status for their own family lose what really matters and bring dishonor on their households. Those who mock and dishonor their neighbors, making sport of them, will fall in shame. Those who trust in idols will find that no God ever heard them and there is no one to come to their aid.

Whatever bombs or terror or malice is out there, there is still a vision. The righteous live by faith. The righteous carry the banner of justice – for our God and for the truth. We do not need to despise our neighbors or lash out for vengeance. We need the light that Rev. Dr. King saw streaming from Christ. We need to live into the vision of God's kingdom so boldly that we can watch as it comes into being. We need to let that light shine out from inside us so that people will stand in wonder and give glory to God. Evil will fall. "The Lord is in the Holy Temple: let all the earth keep silence in God's presence." Amen.

What is God Like?
(Rev. Lucus Keppel)
Isaiah 40:18-23, 28-31; I John 4: 7-16

What does it mean when we talk about the "Sovereignty of God"?

To get at this question, we need to unpack a few things. First, if you're expecting me to say, "God's sovereignty means exactly this…." then, I'm going to need you to put that expectation aside. Like many theological questions, there's not a single, simple answer. Rather, as we discuss a range of answers, we reveal more about the nature of God and how we relate to God. Indeed, I hope that you don't walk away saying, "the question of God's Sovereignty was answered in the book that I read today!" Instead, I encourage you to think of this as being one part in an on-going conversation, with those reading this book today and with those who have gone before in the Church Universal – and the Church to come. We're going to look at historical context, but perhaps your voice will be a part of the historical context to come!

So, what does *sovereignty* mean, anyway? When we talk about sovereignty today, it's usually in the context of sovereign nations – that is, nations that have authority to govern themselves, independent of anyone else. Sovereignty, in this view, sounds very much like a synonym for "independent authority." But does this fit, when talking about God? Given that God created everything, and "nothing in life or death can separate us from the love of God"?[9] Some people take great comfort in God's immediacy, and involvement in their life - and this is good!

On the other hand, how can God NOT be an independent authority? For God is the Potter who shapes the clay,[10] and God is "beyond the reach of human understanding."[11] There's also comfort in this emphasis – that God is in control, that ultimately, God's vision will prevail. Maybe you've felt this tension, a good tension, in the Bible and our understanding of God as a personal being who interacts with us on our level while at the same time being transcendent, all-knowing and all-powerful. Maybe you've noticed that many of our prayers begin with a dual naming of God – I tend to use "Holy and

---

[9] Romans 8:48

[10] Jeremiah 18:1-11

[11] Isaiah 40:22

Beloved God," but we also pray using "Holy and Gracious God" and "Our Father in Heaven" and "Sovereign Source of Salvation," when we're feeling particularly alliterative. These are representations of this tension between God-in-Heaven and God-with-us. If you want to know more about this, the scholarly terms are "God-Transcendent and God-Immanent" – but that's a chapter for another time.

Instead, let's look into this idea of tension a little further. In the Presbyterian Church (USA), we tend not to speak of God's sovereignty alone, but in tension with another attribute of God – God's grace or God's love. Sometimes, the emphasis is more on sovereignty or on grace, but both are present throughout the Reformed church – and, indeed, in the Church Universal as well. The Heidelberg Catechism[12] begins with the question: "What is your only comfort in life& in death?" The answer:

> *That I am not my own, but belong – body and soul, in life and in death – to my faithful Savior, Jesus Christ… He watches over me in such a way that not a hair can fall from my head without the will of my Father in heaven – in fact, all things must work together for my salvation.*[13]

Here, God's sovereignty is emphasized in classic, sweeping terms – everything happens according to God's will – and held in tension with the grace of salvation through Jesus – "all things must work together for my salvation." In a passage from Isaiah 40, God is described both as "inhabiting the horizon"[14] – so far away that the people below look like locusts! – with power over the whole universe. Yet, God is also so close as to be able to "give power to the tired" and "revive the exhausted."[15] Again, we have the tension between God's sovereignty and God's love and care for humanity.

---

[12] Throughout this book, we may refer to Confessions of the church. These confessions are historical statements of the Church Universal, adopted as part of the constitution of the Presbyterian Church (USA). Everyone ordained to ministry in the Presbyterian church (whether as a Ruling Elder, Deacon, or Teaching Elder) vows to be guided by the confessions in their ministry. As Rev. Dr. Amy Plantinga Pauw put it, the "Book of Confessions has no back cover, because we add new historical confessions as the Spirit guides us."

[13] "Heidelberg Catechism. (1563)" In *Book of Confessions*, 4.001. Vol. 1. The Constitution of the Presbyterian Church (USA). (Louisville: Office of the General Assembly of the Presbyterian Church (USA), 2016), 31.

[14] Isaiah 40: 22

[15] Isaiah 40: 29

As uncomfortable as this tension may make us, we people who like simple answers and settled arguments, it is the tension that brings energy to the discussion.

Now, the mechanical-minded among you are nodding your heads already. A spring under tension has potential energy to change to kinetic when it is set free. When you wind your watch, for instance, you're adding energy back to the spring by bringing it into greater tension. The tension between God-with-us and God-in-Heaven provides energy, too! (though God doesn't need to be wound up!)

Another way to look at this is like a swing dance. In a traditional ballroom dance, the couple make a "frame" – a single solid object, by placing their hands on each other's waist and hands, then holding their bodies in tension. That way, one can lead or follow by feeling the pressure exerted by their partner. In swing dance, though, there's no solid frame to move around. Instead, the direction in the dance is provided by the dancers pulling away from each other slightly, turning their arms into a sort of rope under tension. So long as the tension is maintained, the partners on the dancefloor can read each other's direction, and move together.[16]

"So long as that tension is maintained..." That leads us to a historical oddity when it comes to God's sovereign grace – often, sovereignty is emphasized at the expense of grace. When that happens, the tension is lost, and humanity can stumble out of step with God. To better illustrate this, I'm going to turn now to the Reformed theologian Shirley Guthrie:

> *The form of the attributes of God's sovereign majesty... are expressed either... in terms that God is what we are not (infinite, unchangeable)... or that God is what we are at our best, but raised to perfection (most wise, most holy). But when we define God by comparison with ourselves... are we really talking about God or only about ourselves? ...Moreover, if we begin by thinking abstractly of the sovereign majesty of God before we speak of God's love for us in Christ, how can we avoid making God into the image of a human tyrant?*[17]

---

[16] For more on the tension inherent in dance, see the video "Lindy hop connection" by Nikolas Lloyd (aka Lindy Beige) https://youtu.be/Xo36VszY8Nw.

[17] Shirley Guthrie, Jr., "What is God Like?" in *Christian Doctrine*, revised ed. (Louisville: Westminster John Knox Press, 1994), 103.

God as "a human tyrant writ large" is unfortunately an all-too-common understanding. You may have heard of sermons with titles like, "Sinners in the Hands of an Angry God"[18] or "God's Wrath: Eternal Conscious Punishment." Or definitions of God's sovereignty that read "God has the right to do whatever God wants to do."[19] That's what happens when we lose the tension – and stumble out of the dance. We forget that God isn't just God-above-us – but God-with-us, too. That's what our passage from I John is reminding us of: God is love. God does not act contrary to God's nature, which is love[20]. It's not that we love God, but that God first loved us – that God's grace saves us from our stumbling.

You may have noticed that I keep using love and grace interchangeably. They are different, of course, but I'm trying to keep another tension in balance. You see, Luke and Paul talk about God's grace, while Mark, Matthew and John refer to God's love in pretty similar contexts. Turning to the book of confessions, the Scots confession[21] emphasizes that the covenant of grace extends back to Adam. Later, in the Brief Statement of Faith[22], the emphasis is that God's ruling is expressed as love in Christ Jesus, whose life lived and sacrificed for others was vindicated in the resurrection's overruling of death. The Koine Greek word that we translate as "grace" is *charis*[23]. *Charis* originally meant something akin to charm – that's why it's the root of "charisma" – but came to mean in Koine Greek "doing good without reward." God's grace, then, is that God gives Godself to us freely, without expectation, or even ability to pay God back. God's grace is God's love, eternal, and full. God's grace covers our missteps in the dance, and pulls us back into relationship with God. And one of the ways to do that is at the communion table – in the

---

[18] Jonathan Edwards, "Sinners in the Hands of an Angry God." Blue Letter Bible. July 8, 1781. https://www.blueletterbible.org/comm/edwards_jonathan/sermons/sinners.cfm.

[19] John Piper, "Does God Control All Things All the Time?" Desiring God, September 15, 2017. https://www.desiringgod.org/interviews/does-god-control-all-things-all-the-time.

[20] 1 John 4:1-2

[21] "Scots Confession, The (1560)" In *Book of Confessions*, 3.04. Vol. 1. The Constitution of the Presbyterian Church (USA) (Louisville: Office of the General Assembly of the Presbyterian Church (USA), 2016), 12.

[22] "Brief Statement of Faith, A (1991)" In *Book of Confessions*, 11.1-6. Vol. 1. The Constitution of the Presbyterian Church (USA) (Louisville: Office of the General Assembly of the Presbyterian Church (USA), 2016), 311-312.

[23] χάρης (charis)

sacrament of the eucharist. Eu-*charis*-t. The table of good grace. The table of communion with the love of God.

When we believe truly that we belong to God's sovereign grace, we can get into the swing of the dance. We can share God's love and grace with others, secure that God will lead us where we are most needed, and will pick us up when we fall, fill us with energy to fly across the dancefloor like eagles wheeling in the sky. For nothing in life or in death can separate us from the love of God.[24]

May God-in-heaven lead you in the dance of life. May the Christ, God-with-us, fill us with love for God and each other. May the Holy Spirit remind us of the tension that causes us to fly like eagles and never grow weary of the dance. Amen.

---

[24] Romans 8:38-39

Confession of Sin

Anger or Righteousness?
(Rev. Elana Levy)
Psalm 37:1-11, 14-17, 27-28a, 39-40;
Romans 12:19-21; James 1:19-21

Thirty years ago, "The Princess Bride" was released in theatres. I know what you're thinking – "inconceivable!" – but it's true. It is a movie of heroes, giants, villains, wizards, and true love on a course that never did run smooth. Early in the movie, the main character, Westley, meets a Spanish swordsman of incredible skill. They start as enemies, but Inigo Montoya takes a moment to tell his life's story. He says that when he was eleven,

> *"My father was slaughtered by a six-fingered man. He was a great sword-maker, my father. When the six-fingered man appeared and requested a special sword, my father took the job. He slaved a year before it was done… The six-fingered man returned and demanded it, but at one-tenth his promised price. My father refused. Without a word, the six-fingered man slashed him through the heart. I loved my father. So, naturally, I challenged his murderer to a duel. I failed.... [W]hen I was strong enough, I dedicated my life to the study of fencing. So the next time we meet, I will not fail. I will go up to the six-fingered man and say, 'Hello. My name is Inigo Montoya. You killed my father. Prepare to die.'"* [25]

Inigo Montoya was a child who witnessed something horrifying. His father was cheated and murdered and, as a young child, Inigo was not strong enough to avenge his father's death. That moment was one of great loss, but also deep shame for him. And he gave his life to become a swordsman. By the time the movie takes place, he seems to be in his mid-thirties. He's still desperately searching for the man who killed his father, but he's paying the bills working for a man who believes himself to be a Sicilian criminal mastermind. Getting nowhere in his quest for vengeance, he has become a frustrated, bitter drunk.

---

[25] *The Princess Bride*, directed by Rob Reiner, screenplay by William Goldman, featuring Cary Elwes and Mandy Patinkin (Act III Communications, 1987), DVD, MGM Home Entertainment, 2001.

Inigo Montoya's moment of vengeance does come near the end of the film and, despite being terribly wounded, he confronts and defeats the six-fingered man saying again and again, "Hello. My name is Inigo Montoya. You killed my father. Prepare to die."[26] It feels like a great triumph for the heroes, but there's this interesting moment afterwards where Inigo pauses and reflects, "[It] is very strange. I have been in the revenge business so long. Now that it's over, I don't know what to do with the rest of my life."[27]

Anger is a force to be reckoned with and before we know what's happened, it can swallow up so much more than we realize. Considering how powerful that anger can be, it's interesting how often we describe it using images of fire. Anger burns hotly within us. We can be consumed with thoughts of revenge. We get all fired up when we're yelling about something. And when we're so angry that we're about to go berserk, we might say that smoke is coming out of our ears or that we're seeing red. Like fire, anger can easily flare out of control and threaten to harm all in its path (including the angry one).

The thing about anger is that it taps into one of the most primal parts of our brains, sometimes called the reptilian brain. It's where that fight or flight impulse comes from and it's part of our survival instinct. That means that if we feel threatened enough and angry enough, our primal brain is able to hijack the rest of our brain. It can cause us to act without us thinking it through or even seeming to choose what we're doing. When we see red, it can get to the point where it feels like something else took control of us. If we keep feeding that fire, if we nurse our grudges and hold onto our pain and anger, we can lose control and then we can lose everything.

But this is not a sermon about the great power of anger and our unfortunate helplessness. There is a long road between something that angers us and the primal brain taking control and causing us to see red. James reminds us to, "be quick to listen, slow to speak, slow to anger; for your anger does not produce God's righteousness." James wants us to see that our anger is a tool that God gave to us -not a burden, not a sin by itself. The power that we feel when we are angry is not why God gave us the ability to be angry.

We affirm with scripture that we were created in God's image, that we are truly God's children. Anger is a part of that. The Bible speaks over and over again about God's anger, God's wrath. God gets angry because who we are

---

[26] Ibid.

[27] Ibid.

and what we do matter to God. God guides us and teaches us and chastises us because God wants us to live in love and harmony with one another.

So where does anger fit into that? Well, here is how I would define anger: anger is our automatic response to injustice, whether it happens to us or to someone else. Think about things that you get angry about – politicians taking bribes, people being murdered in their homes, someone cutting you off on the freeway. Each of these things hit us hard because that's not how we believe that people should behave. Politicians should vote their conscience and not special interests – corruption is unjust. People should be safe to live their lives in their own homes and communities – senseless loss of life is unjust. People driving recklessly…well, they're jerks. It's unfair to endanger me and my car because you feel a little impatient and crazy! Anger is a warning light in our minds alerting us to something that is wrong. And that fight or flight adrenaline and power and energy that we feel – that's our mind and body preparing itself to do something about it. We are physically built to fight injustice and to work for good.

This might sound over-simplified: see a bad thing, internal bat-signal goes off, fix a bad thing. But that's how the system was designed to work. The problem comes when we feed the anger and fan those flames. The problem comes when we don't use that energy to make things better – we use it to focus in on what made us angry. Then we get bitter and wrathful and obsessive. Then we stew and fume and sabotage others and cut ourselves off from the hope and the possibility of life. Then we become Inigo Montoya and don't notice that 20 plus years have gone by and we never had the time to build something meaningful for our own lives. When anger turns to wrath, when anger becomes our home and not a means of moving forward, then we have crossed the line into sin.

The question becomes: anger or righteousness? Revenge or justice? Because after a certain point, if we believe that we have to take everything into our own hands – if we believe that our anger is the only thing that will bring about true justice…then we have lost faith and our anger has become our god. In the Romans passage, Paul admonishes his readers to never avenge themselves, but to leave room for the wrath of God. Then he quotes Deuteronomy 32, "Vengeance is mine, I will repay, says the Lord." If vengeance belongs to the Lord, that means that it does not belong to us. Justice wants to get back what we are owed, to try to restore what was lost. Vengeance, by contrast, doesn't care about what is just. Vengeance wants the other person to suffer because we have suffered. In some cases, vengeance can never be satisfied. But what God has said, what Paul is bringing to our attention is that we are not called to be the agents of ultimate punishment.

We are not the ones who will bring forward the consequences of the evil in each one's heart. Only God can do that. So if we trust God to repay the wicked, if we trust God to heal our wounds, then our lives will not be dominated by anger and hatred and vengeance.

In Christ, we are free to live and grow and explore new hopes and new challenges, building up where we are able. With this freedom, we can feed our enemies and we can give them something to drink because, "by doing this [we] heap burning coals on their heads." If anger is a fire and its coals are hottest and strongest clustered together – if this angry fire becomes stronger when it is fed more and more fuel, then what is the best way forward? Surely, if we heap burning coals over someone's head, the coals will burn hot for a moment and then they will fall away and cool down. We can transform our anger into an act of compassion for even the most wicked – even those who, "bring down the poor and needy, [those who] kill those who walk uprightly." Maybe the Spirit will work through us to turn their hearts. Maybe the coals we heap on their heads will dislodge some of the embers from their own anger and hatred. And that is a miracle.

When God strengthens us to equip ourselves with anger, then we can, "be still before the Lord, and wait patiently for God." Then we won't have to worry about people who do evil things and seem to have all the fortune and the luck. Because as Psalm 37 reminds us and Jesus echoed in the beatitudes: "the meek shall inherit the earth." It is the humble – those who seem lowly and powerless – who can lean on the strength of their faith and trust in the Lord to release their anger and live in love. That is the kingdom of heaven that Christ is building all around us, even as we speak. That is the reality that you and I can live into more and more each day. The psalmist encourages us, "depart from evil, and do good; so you shall abide forever. For the Lord loves justice; God will not forsake the faithful." It doesn't say do it all perfectly. It doesn't say, "try to do good, but if you mess up or it's too hard, it's probably alright to keep doing the same old sinning." We can't fully and finally depart from evil – but we can depart every day, as often as we need, leaning on Christ each step of the way.

Even though Inigo Montoya gave up 20 years of his life, he started a new path at the end of the movie. No matter how much anger and hatred have taken hold on your life, there is always time to let it go and to practice this new life in Christ. And so, friends, be directed by your anger, but not dominated by it. Be patient for the Lord to act, trusting that God accomplishes justice even if we don't see it in our lifetimes. Use this faith and this hope to let your life become beautiful, surrounded by love, and trust in the kingdom of heaven. Amen.

Testing God
(Revs. Levy & Keppel)
Judges 6:36-40; Daniel 3 (Select Verses)

In this sermon, both of us took on the roles of characters from the Bible, placed in conversation with each other. Lucus wrote and performed as Gideon, while Elana wrote and performed as Azariah (not Abednego!)

Gideon:

> I, Gideon, least among the Manasseh family, will rescue our people from our oppressors, the Midianites. At least, that's what the messenger of God told me one morning, while I was working at my Dad's place. Well, sort of. At first, he greeted me with a hearty, "The Lord is with you, Mighty Warrior!" while I was hiding the fact that I had food from the Midianite spies. Not surprisingly, I snapped at him: "With all due respect, *good sir*, if the Lord is with us, why has all of this happened? Where are all the amazing works and miracles that our ancestors talked about? Why is Midian allowed to overpower us?"
>
> You see, I don't do much of anything without proof. I know that the wheat that I thresh out will be ground into fine flour for my food, because I've done it enough times to be certain. I know that the sun moves a little each day, charting out the year in the sky, because I've watched it enough years now to be certain. So, when I hear my dad tell stories of things like water coming out of rocks, and walls tumbling down, and bread from heaven – I'm not quite as certain. I've never seen these things myself.
>
> Yet, the messenger – the angel – didn't laugh at me or make fun of me for wanting a sign. Instead, he said, "Because I'm with you, you'll be able to defeat all of the Midianites as if they were just a single person." Then, he went on to shoot fire out of a rock and vanish before my eyes. That's the level of awesome I encountered when I asked for a sign of God to be with me. And so, it's no wonder that now, facing an army of not only Midianites, but Amalekites and others, that I again want a sign of God's presence. The Lord provides a sign to reassure my heart that yes, no matter what God has called me to do, God is there to help me do it.

Ok, God: here's a fleece, on the threshing floor. Make the dew fall on it but keep the floor dry. Then I'll know you're with me, that we're doing the right thing – that we have a chance of surviving in the morning.

Azariah:

My name is not Abednego. No matter how many times they call me that – it's not my name. It means "servant of Nebo," a Babylonian god (*spits*). My real name is Azariah – it means "The LORD helps." When my parents named me, they honored the strength and the love of the one, true God and I have dedicated my life to this walk of faith. I only thank the LORD that they did not live to see this day: Jerusalem conquered, the Temple destroyed, the people scattered and tyrannized in exile. Babylon is not our home, but here we live oppressed by the hours, yearning to be free.

We were an important family back in Israel, educated, faithful, and strong. And that's why Nebuchadnezzar forced me to be in his royal court. He picked the best and brightest of us and forced us to endure 3 years of nonsense education – predicting the future with animal guts, how to worship false idols, the greatness of all-powerful Babylon (*spits*). We will not let them erase us, destroy our faith, brainwash us into shame. So we hold on to what we can to keep our faith alive: we cannot offer sacrifice in the Temple, we cannot look to the stronghold of Jerusalem, but we can follow God's commandments in our hearts and in our homes. The king can control our lives, our work, our country, but he cannot control our consciences and our hearts. We can live sacred lives no matter what these barbarians try to force on us. We pray to the one true God together. We refuse meat offered to idols. We live lives of virtue, trusting that God will deliver us.

When everything has been taken from you, you would give anything to keep what is most precious. Nebuchadnezzar says we will die if we do not worship his false god. I say – whether we live or whether we die, we belong to the one true God. Our lives do not matter – only God's justice, truth, and faithfulness. Anyone who challenges the God of Israel will find out what that means. We don't need to test God because only God is God and the LORD is always watching.

Gideon:

> Look, Azariah, I know that God is always watching. That's how I know that God will answer me when I ask for signs. Because anyone can say that they're from God, bringing a message – but only God can provide the proof to be certain. How can I possibly face the Midianite army – with only three hundred soldiers – without knowing that this is truly what God wants us to do? After all, I have time this evening to pray and ask for God's sign, so I should take it, and make absolutely certain. While I appreciate that you're willing to honor God's commands and risk your own life in the process, I'm facing something new. God's asking me to do something specific, and I think specific instructions need to be tested. How else could I know if the message is coming from God, or from a mischievous spirit – or, worse, an entity that wants to see Israel fall in ruin?

This is a very important point: God knows that when God asks us to do difficult things, we need to know that it is God doing the asking. Sometimes, that comes from knowing our scriptures – I don't need to ask God for a sign if I'm contemplating dishonoring my parents or ignoring the Sabbath. I know right from wrong, then, because God has taught us. But when God calls me – me, Gideon, least of Manasseh – to do something like send away the majority of our army because God will provide – yeah, then I want specific proof. I'll ask God to do something difficult – and then to do it again, differently – just to be certain that it's God doing the asking.

Indeed, our ancestor Moses asked God for signs that the burning bush was actually God! And God provided that sign, even allowing Moses to see God's glorious face. Joseph, too, was able to prove that God's messages were the ones sent, because Joseph was able to truly interpret dreams. When I asked God for yet another sign that God was the one telling me to do these strange things, God sent a dream message and an interpretation – and caused me to overhear both!

So, I will keep testing the messages to see if they're of God, because God provides safety and assurance of God's presence through these tests. I have the time to ask God for these signs, and God is gracious, providing them as needed. For God is as reliable and steadfast as the mountains and the sea – and to not ask for proof is asking to be deceived.

Azariah:

I never really thought about it that way, Gideon. Here in Babylon, Nebuchadnezzar is the one who is testing God. He's being ruthless and violent and discounting God's power and might. Moses himself said, "do not put the LORD your God to the test." Don't challenge God as though God's arm is too short to save or God is too weak to hear us call. Who are we to say what God can and cannot do – what God will or will not do? It is my calling to serve, to live as righteous a life as I can, and to trust that God is holding it together.

I get that you want a sign to be really clear about specific instructions, but we don't always get a sign when we want one. In those times, we do what's right anyway. We keep praying and we keep moving forward because God will guide us if we keep the faith. Me and my friends, we went into that furnace peacefully. We didn't resist. We didn't have weapons and escape plans. But our faith was so dangerous to the king that he called some of his strongest guards and they tied us up with ropes so that we could scarcely move. And the fire was so hot, Gideon, you don't know… It was so hot that those strong guards perished when they threw us in.

Nebuchadnezzar had wanted us to fall down to worship him and his gods – we fell down in the furnace, but we would not fall down on our faith. Ya know, I guess that's really what we're talking about. Testing God doesn't mean that we think we're the ones who can judge God. You're saying that testing God means discerning what God wants us to do – live faithfully. Because you're right – if we know what the right thing is to do, we ought to do it. And if we have time to discern something more complicated in prayer, then we should take it. But sometimes in the moment, all we can do is test our own hearts, hold on to the truth, and keep walking forward. I did, and God saved my life. You did, and God gave you victory. We don't always win, but we do know that if we keep the faith, God will see us through. Praise the LORD.

Gideon:

The LORD's name be praised.

Assurance of Pardon

Love Will Seek You
(Rev. Elana Levy)
Song of Songs 3:1-4a; Luke 15:8-10; 1 John 4:16b-21

A lost coin, a lost love, a lost brother or sister: nobody likes to lose things, but it's something that we're all kinda good at. Sure, some of us are better at losing things than others, but given enough time and distraction, we'll lose just about anything – no matter how important it is. And we look forward to that glorious day when our, "light shall break forth like the dawn" and that lost bauble will return to its rightful place by our side. And there will be much rejoicing. There is nothing like the joy when something that was lost returns home again.

William Still was born in 1821 in New Jersey, born free, though his parents had both suffered as slaves. He was the youngest of 18 children. He didn't have much in the way of formal education, but he taught himself to read and write. In 1847 when he was 26 years old, he started working for the Pennsylvania Society for the Abolition of Slavery. Founded in 1775, it was the oldest abolitionist society in the country and Benjamin Franklin once served as its president. William Still became the chairman of the "Vigilance Committee," which provided direct aid to slaves who had escaped and reached Philadelphia. He raised money to help runaways and make their journeys easier. He even helped Harriet Tubman financially. In fact, William Still is sometimes called the "Father of the Underground Railroad." He helped as many as 800 slaves escape and he opened his home as a hiding place for them. Not only that – he got to know every slave that he met and he recorded their stories. He knew that their lives and their struggles mattered, and he was determined not to let their lives be lost to history. In 1872, Still published a book of their stories – one of the few early histories that portrayed slaves as having courage and daring and fortitude.[28]

But before all this – before he was the chairman of the Vigilance Committee and a bold rescuer of others, he was a simple clerk. And in 1850, when he was 29 years old, he met a man named Peter. Peter was an escaped slave, telling William his story. Peter said that his father had bought his way out of slavery in Maryland, but his mother had not been able to do so. Many years before, Charity had tried to escape from slavery in Maryland, but she was caught along with her four children. For her next attempt, she took only her

---

[28] "William Still," in *Wikipedia: The Free Encyclopedia*, Wikimedia Foundation Inc., updated 2 August 2018, https://en.wikipedia.org/wiki/William_Still

2 daughters with her and managed to reach her husband Levin in New Jersey. Tragically left behind, Peter explained that he and his brother Levin, Jr. were eventually sold to slave masters in Kentucky and then resold to a man in Alabama. Levin, Jr. was caught visiting his wife without permission from his slave owner. He was whipped so severely that he died.[29]

At the age of 50, Peter managed to escape, and he came to the Pennsylvania Society for the Abolition of Slavery to find his mother and father or any other members of his family. William listened to Peter's story with shock and amazement. After learning how Levin, Jr. had died, William proclaimed, "What if I told you I was your brother!" Peter's story was one that William knew very well because it was his parent's story, too. Their parents had struggled for years to find and free their two oldest sons, but they were lost – seemingly forever. After Peter met William, he was reunited with his mother after a separation of 42 years and he met all of the rest of his 16 brothers and sisters that he didn't even know existed.[30]

I cannot even imagine the miracle of that moment – the unbelievable joy, the shock, the disbelief, the overflowing hearts. And neither of them knew – neither of them even suspected that they might have been who the other was looking for, a restoration of family where it must have seemed impossible.

When we lose things or even people, we can find ourselves lost in despair or we can find ourselves becoming seekers. In our passage from the Song of Songs, we hear the voice of the bride to be. Some believe her speech is the retelling of a dream – others that of a sleepless night. Either way, she wants the one whom her soul loves. Finding him again is her sole focus and she will not rest until they are together again. She looks for him, she calls for him, she even bothers the night guards in the city who, I'm guessing, probably don't really care about this lovesick young woman. But she is devoted, and she is clear in her intention – she will be reunited and when she found him, she, "held him, and would not let him go." Her satisfaction comes from her love.

Or let's look at the woman from the Gospel lesson this morning. Certainly, she doesn't love her money as much as the bride to be loves her fiancée (at least I hope she doesn't!). But she will search her house, sweeping the floor, lighting an oil lamp to look in all the dark corners, behind and underneath everything until that which is lost is found once more. And her joy is so great

---

[29] Ibid

[30] Ibid

that she has to share it with everyone she knows – she publishes the news abroad. Tell everyone – party at my house. I have found what was lost!

Losing, seeking, finding, and celebrating – we can understand what this means. The heartache, the yearning, the cautious hope, and the wild jubilation. What is interesting about the lost coin story is that Jesus tells us that's exactly what the joy is like in heaven when one sinner repents – a change of heart and a change of life. We are the coin. We are the lost love. We are the lost brother, the lost parents, that lost family. We don't cause ourselves to be found. We don't twinkle extra hard in the corner of the room or transmit GPS coordinates to the loved ones that seek us out. God is the seeker and we are the found. And that means that we are not defined by our lost-ness. Being lost is never the sum total of who we are. We are God's children and we are all sisters and brothers. Just imagine telling someone how lost you feel to sin, how alone, how unreachable, only to have them say as William Still did, "What if I told you I was your brother!" "What if I told you I was your sister!" What if isolation is a myth and the idea of being unforgivable, irredeemable, hopeless – what if that is a lie that we don't have to believe anymore?

Because when we look at 1 John, we find bold words of hope. It is simple enough to say that "God is love" and to ascribe great and holy and wonderful things to an untouchable, unreachable God. It is another thing entirely to say, "those who abide in love abide in God, and God abides in them." We may think we are lost to sin, but we are living in love, which means that we live in God and God lives in us. How can we be lost when God is our home? How can you be lost when you know that love will seek you?

And so, let us find sisters and brothers in unexpected places. Let us unmask sin for all of its weakness, grasping hard to the power and love of God. And let us never forget that our repentance on earth means a radiant, boisterous, gleeful, outrageous party in heaven and it is part of our calling to fill our Lord and Savior with gladness. May you celebrate your home in the Lord and in this family of faith every day of your life. Amen.

Refining the Soul
(Rev. Lucus Keppel)
Malachi 3:1-6, 14-17; 1 Peter 1: 3-7, 13-16

Picture this: You are in ancient Egypt, taking a stroll along the banks of the Nile. Your sandal-covered feet are protected from the hot rocks in the midday sun, but the green grass beyond the riverbanks is cool and refreshing. The river twists and turns as you walk along its edge, and you stop for a moment at the very edge of the river bank. You take off your large-brimmed hat – a requirement for life in the ancient world – and dip it in the river water for a refreshing cool. As you reach down, you notice little sparkling flakes in the sand, glinting as the river water turns suddenly. Excitedly, you gather the sandy mixture in your hat, and start spilling the water out of it, carrying away the fertile soil and sand mixture, and leaving behind the golden flakes. Congratulations – you've found natural gold!

Now, you haven't found much of it, admittedly, but gold is a pretty amazing substance, especially in the ancient world. It is soft – so soft that it can be hammered into exceedingly thin sheets that lose no luster or color. In nature, it never tarnishes, and it takes extremely potent acids and bases to dissolve it. It is sometimes mixed with other metals in an ore – and often, those other metals are also highly valued – silver, copper and even lead. Because gold can be found naturally, like in the scenario we just imagined, people in the ancient world were very familiar with it – and wanted more of it. After all, in civilizations from the Sumerians to the Aztecs, its purity and eternal shine reminded people of the world of the divine!

By the time of the Kingdom of Israel, gold was pretty well-established as the universal means of transferring money – but it was so valuable that it couldn't easily be used for small transactions. In fact, one of the words for "pure gold" in Hebrew literally means "locked gold"[31] – as in, if this is being sold, all the other stores must be locked up, because there's no way to compete. Instead of using gold for everyday transactions, then, the kingdom of Israel used silver, measured in units of weight known as shekels. A biblical shekel is about a half-ounce (14.1g), and a shekel of silver was usually the equivalent of four Greek Drachma or Roman Denarii, or about four days of work for the average laborer. Every year, every Jewish male adult gave the Temple a half-shekel of silver in dues – and this had to be paid in Jewish coins, no matter who was in control of Judea at the time. It's no surprise that the

---

[31] סָגוּר (segor) – the locked-up thing.

ancient Hebrew word for silver – *kesef*[32] – is the modern Hebrew word for money in general.

The ancients, then, actually had more daily contact with precious metals than we do. Not only did they use metals for daily transactions in the marketplaces, but they would also be more familiar with where they came from, since land owners would often smelt the metals from their own land. That's one of the reasons why it's one of the common biblical images for forgiveness and atonement, and at the core of what having a change of heart meant.

One of the earliest references to refining in the bible is in Proverbs 17:3 – "The crucible is for silver, the furnace is for gold, but the Lord refines the heart." Now, if you're looking this up on your own, most translations have "the Lord tests the heart" – but this usage of "test" really does mean "refine" in modern English. You see, silver and gold ore need to be heated to just the right temperature to melt the pure metal away from the dross and slag. Too low, and they won't melt – too high, and the dross will melt, too. So, to make sure that the temperature of the furnace was correct, the ancients needed to test it. They obviously didn't have access to an infrared thermometer, but they did recognize that certain clays and metals melted at certain temperatures and would test the temp by sacrificing a little of these materials. By making a crucible out of known clay, they could also use its color to test the temperature. For this reason, "testing" silver meant melting the metal out of its ore, and then blowing off the white lead-oxide dross as it cooled.

What does all of this tell us about God's action in refining our soul? As you can tell, it's a lot more involved than it seems at first glance. In his letter to the churches of Asia Minor, Peter offers an initial word of encouragement:

> *There is wonderful joy ahead, even though you must endure many trials for a little while. These trials will show that your faith is genuine. It is being tested as fire tests and purifies gold – though your faith is far more precious than mere gold.*[33]

Here, we again see this "test and purify" construction. Remember, this means "refine." Given that, it seems that Peter is saying that if we face difficulty and danger in this world, our faith can stand it. Not only can our faith stand the test, but as the dross – the sin, the hatred, the dehumanization, the

---

[32] כֶּסֶף (kesef) – silver/money

[33] 1 Peter 1:6-7 (NLT)

disconnection from each other and God – will be left behind, or perhaps even blown away by the breath of God.

We see this metaphor of metallurgic refinement all through the Hebrew Bible, too. The books of Proverbs, Isaiah, Zechariah and of course, Malachi, have explicit references to refinement of the heart by God. Let's take a closer look at a Malachi passage, from chapter 3. Early Christian writers saw Malachi as the last of the Hebrew prophets, though there are writings from after his time in the Bible. By Malachi's day, it wasn't enough to stand in the streets – or even in the temple – and state to the people, "Thus sayeth the Lord." Many had copied this style, and many were ignored, or dismissed. Malachi's style is different – he uses almost a Q&A format that grabbed people's attention:

> *You said, 'Serving God is useless. What do we gain by keeping his obligation, or by walking around as mourners before the Lord of heavenly forces? So now we consider the arrogant fortunate. Moreover, those doing evil are built up; they test God and escape.*[34]

In this way, Malachi serves as a mirror to the people, presenting their own arguments, and refuting them one by one. It's a sophisticated technique, allowing people to provide answers and leading them to draw their own conclusion – "Then those revering the Lord, each and every one, spoke among themselves. The Lord paid attention and listened to them." You see? In his way, Malachi was revealing to the people the refining that God was already doing among them – and would continue to do:

> *The messenger of the covenant in whom you take delight is coming, says the Lord of heavenly forces. Who can endure the day of his coming? Who can withstand his appearance? He is like the refiner's fire or the fuller's soap. He will sit as a refiner and purifier of silver. He will purify the Levites and refine them like gold and silver. They will belong to the Lord, presenting a righteous offering.*[35]

Here, the refining is offered in the future, as a thing to come. But to prepare, Malachi is encouraging people to turn back to God, to cease doing the things that cause harm in the world, everything from adultery to telling falsehoods, to cheating people out of their hard-earned silver, and "brushing aside the

---

[34] Malachi 3:14-15 (CEB)

[35] Malachi 3:1b-3 (CEB)

foreigner." In Lent, as we continue to examine ourselves for the tarnish of sin, this warning carries a real weight with it.

Lucus demonstrating color-changing grace in worship at Corona United Presbyterian Church in Corona, NM. (2014)

There's a really neat way to demonstrate this idea, without needing a foundry. Remember that Malachi refers to both refiner's fire and fuller's soap? Using his reference to soap a bit loosely, we can demonstrate the concept. First, we fill a container about halfway with a purple liquid that represents the human condition – red sin mixed with blue grace. It's a purple life. And it fits nicely with the liturgical color of Lent, which is also purple! If we turn away from God, embracing sin, we add a bit of this lemon juice – which turns the condition liquid more and more red. But God's grace – green, for grace – purifies us to be pure blue. You see, no matter how often we pour the purple liquids together – sharing ideas, trying to escape our sin – we can't eliminate it. But Jesus, filled with grace, refines our soul – bringing out the love and grace that God had intended. The more that grace is active in us, the more we can share with each other in community![36]

---

[36] If you wish to replicate this demonstration for yourself, take a red cabbage and boil it for about 20 minutes, until the water takes on a strong color (usually purple, but if you have acidic or basic water, it may be more blue or red). This liquid is a

After all, as Peter reminds us, it is good to continue rejoicing together! Wrapped up in the metaphor of refining the soul is the idea that our faith is, at our core, pure. No matter how much the toxic lead of sin has wrapped around it. That's what it means that we were originally created in the image of God! And even if we have fallen from this perfect state, Peter reminds us that our inheritance in God is kept in heaven, "pure and undefiled, beyond the reach of change and decay."[37] This inheritance is ours, not because of what we have done, but because of Jesus' life, death, and resurrection. And so, this golden faith is still within us, preserved no matter what occurs, becoming even more visible as the heat is turned up around us. Peter is not telling us to seek out the testing, the furnace – no, instead, he is reminding us that if we find ourselves in the furnace, we will glow with the heat, and find ourselves showing the faith of God all the more clearly. Even if we tarnish again – and again – and again – God's grace is enough to purify us again, and again, and again.

May you always recognize the difference between filth and faith, knowing that God wants you to be whole and at peace. May you be filled with joy even through times of intense heat, knowing that Christ is leading you through. May your soul be refined so that the Spirit of God will blow away your dross, and fill you with pure, golden faith. Amen.

---

natural PH indicator. When mixed with acidic lemon juice or vinegar, it will turn red. When mixed with basic/alkaline liquids, like ammonia, it will turn blue – and then green. To make the green grace, I mixed ammonia with red cabbage water, diluting it enough to make a little of the green liquid counteract a lot of the red PH. Try to mix them in small amounts until you get a handle on how much it takes to change the color! Also – you'll want to have sealed containers for all the liquids, as they can be pretty smelly if left open in the sanctuary.

[37] I Peter 1:4b

Alive in Christ Jesus
(Rev. Elana Levy)
John 20:1-18; Romans 6:1-11

When Jesus died, there were Roman soldiers standing guard, there were criminals on either side of him, there were chief priests and scribes and elders who mocked and misunderstood him. There was a crowd of people looking on at the spectacle. The twelve betrayed and abandoned him; the multitudes whom he had fed and wowed from town to town were nowhere to be found. But standing before the cross was Mary Magdalene, Mary mother of James and Joseph, the mother of the sons of Zebedee, Jesus's mother Mary, Jesus' aunt, Mary the wife of Clopas, Salome, and the beloved disciple. After Jesus' death, they were joined by Joseph of Arimathea and Nicodemus in caring for his body, trying to cover the marks of hatred and violence with a swaddling of perfume and love.

On Good Friday, we often sing "Were You There When They Crucified My Lord?"[38] Looking at each of the Gospel accounts, we see that so many of the faithful wouldn't be there. They couldn't bear to watch Jesus die – they couldn't bear the thought of life without him. Even those who were there – perhaps they wanted most to be together with Jesus for the last few moments of his life. Maybe they were only there to say goodbye.

As Jesus was dying, Luke's Gospel tells us that the sun was eclipsed – the grief of this found family, drawn together by no less than the Son of God come to earth – was even echoed by the heavens and the earth. It was, indeed, a dark day. And as Jesus commended his spirit into the waiting hands of his Father, all they could do is watch and grieve. They had left everything to follow him. What would they do now? Where would they go? Would the Romans come after them next?

We meet Mary Magdalene, early Sunday morning, drawn to the tomb. Magdalene was saved by Jesus from 7 demons who had tormented her. She was not, as some traditions have it, a prostitute. She was a woman of some means and she financially supported Jesus and his ministry. Of all the women that followed Jesus, she was the foremost, and so it is no wonder that she returned to his side. She weeps for her savior, she weeps for (what she

---

[38] "Were you there" (No. 228) in *Glory to God: The Presbyterian Hymnal* (Louisville: Westminster John Knox Press, 2013).

assumes) was a graveyard robbery – adding insult to injury. Before she saw the angels, she had lost everything.

The darkest times, for Mary, for any of us, are when things have gone so catastrophically wrong that we can't see any way out of it. We can't even imagine a way for things to be good again – or even marginally improved. These impossibly deep valleys can grow to become a chasm – an abyss that sucks the life and hope away from our present, even as they start to drag away more and more moments of our future.

I once knew a young girl, I'll call her Molly, who was really struggling. I was a counselor at a summer camp. I volunteered to work with 9-11 year-olds because they're old enough to puzzle through ideas and problems, but they're not so old that they're too cool to be goofy. The week that Molly was at camp, we started out the same way – with the silly getting to know your games and ice breakers – but she was different from the other girls. Sometimes she would play along with everyone else, laughing and having a good time, and other times she was withdrawn and irritable. A pleasant conversation snapped into biting someone's head off in the blink of an eye. Bless her heart, she had caught that dreaded ailment that all kids must face and all parents dread – she was a teenager. But she caught it early and she caught it bad. Every emotion that she had was the rawest, most intense version she had ever experienced. And you could see her start to yell at someone, realize that she didn't want to be yelling, and then run off embarrassed and ashamed.

After a few days, Molly decided that no one wanted to be her friend; no one understood her; no one cared. One evening, after she had had a rather nasty blow up with another camper, I went over to talk to her. It wasn't too long before her tent mates came in, too – sitting quietly at a bit of a respectful distance. She started to talk about how hurt and sad and confused that she was. She was having a hard time at school, things were rough at home, and her grandmother – her favorite relative – had just died. It was all too much. With tears streaming down her face, she apologized to me for behaving so badly, for hurting everyone, and making them hate her. And every single one of those girls came closer to her. Those that could touched her back or her arm and they all said, "we don't hate you." "We're sorry things are so hard for you." One or two of them told her about how hard it was for them when they lost family members and loved ones. They said that it wasn't easy, but that her heart would heal in time.

Why was Molly crying? Why was Mary crying? Because it was impossible, right? Because too much had gone wrong, because there was no more room for hope to grow, because no one could possibly understand. But Christ is risen. Christ is alive and the life that he lost was given for us. Christ was raised for us so that we might be raised with him – so that we might walk in newness of life.

Every sorrow, every hardship and calamity, every evil and sin in this world is answered by Christ in his dying and rising. If we fear that we suffer alone and that God does not care about our pain – see, Christ took on the worst pain the world had to offer in body and mind and spirit and yet he lives! He rose and so we will rise up. If we fear that we are tainted and bad, too full of sin to ever stand before the glory and beauty of our God – see, Christ is a sacrifice of purification, a sin offering that removes our impurity and cleanses us to be embraced forever more in the arms of God! Christ rose and so we will rise up. If we search our consciences and convince ourselves that we have done wrong and could never be loved or forgiven – see, Christ took on our guilt and accepted the penalty for all time. But God directed our end to be life and not death! Because he lives, we will live. If we fear that death has the final word and that we are truly lost – see, Christ died on the cross, descended into hell, and broke the chains of its gates. His is the final victory! He rose from death so that we will rise up. If we fear that evil is too powerful and that the meek and the good can only fail and fall away – see, Christ conquered evil and raises up goodness to eternity.

Christ is our hope. As the apostle Paul tells us, "If we have died with Christ, we believe that we will also live with him."[39] The promise of faith born from Easter morning is a simple one: live! Live with Christ! Do not despair, do not give up, but hold onto the hope of life in Christ whatever you face. Mary thought there was no other way. Molly thought no one could love her. The power of Christ's saving death and miraculous new life is that there are no dead ends for us. God in Christ in Spirit is blowing through our world, bringing new life to the wilderness, gathering us into communities of work and worship, changing the world with the light that shines through any obstacle. Be not afraid, friends, for we are alive in Christ Jesus. Hallelujah! Amen.

---

[39] Romans 6

Passing the Peace

Campfire
(Rev. Lucus Keppel)
Jeremiah 29: 1, 4-7; Luke 17: 11-19

There's something special about a campfire after the sun has gone down. It doesn't really matter how hot it is outside, or who you're camping with - the light and warmth of the campfire is always welcome. It's familiar. It's like a portable home. As a Scout, we had to learn how to build fires safely, whether it was dry as a bone, or so soaking wet that we had to hold a tarp over the fire while it was starting up! There're a few important things to keep in mind: first, you have to arrange the wood. You can't just dump a mix of sizes and shapes into the fire pit – well, you CAN, but it doesn't catch quickly nor burn evenly. What you want to do is make a lean-to or a log cabin with your wood, so that big logs support smaller branches, which support twigs and kindling. Fires start small and grow – and arranging the wood ahead of time is your best way of keeping the fire manageable after it's been started.

Next, you need to apply heat – from the friction of rubbing sticks together, if you're primitive camping, or from a match or lighter if you're using tech to make life easier! Once the kindling goes, the fire will produce its own heat, but every campfire must be started by applying heat in some way. Lastly, a fire needs air – oxygen – to burn. The more oxygen available, the hotter and brighter the fire will burn, and the faster the fire will use up its fuel. That's why you fan coals or blow into the fire after adding new logs – to jumpstart the process again. So, for any fire, you need to first arrange wood, then apply heat, and make sure to keep a steady supply of air!

With that fire going, it's like you've got a piece of home with you, no matter where you are. Imagine how important that comfort would be if you were exiled like the Judeans and Israelites! That's the situation we find in Jeremiah 29. Four years have passed since the exile in Babylon began, and though rebellious sentiment is certainly running through Judah, the Babylonians are simply too powerful for a rebellion to succeed. The skilled artisans, many of the priests, and the political families have all been exiled into Babylon, leaving the unskilled laborers behind. Jeremiah, though a prophet, has not been exiled, and is writing from Jerusalem after the temple has been destroyed. Instead of inciting rebellion in the capital of their captor's empire, Jeremiah tells the people to settle in. "Marry, plant gardens, and seek the *shalom*[40] of

---

[40] שָׁלוֹם (shalom) – Peace, wholeness

the city where you are exiled,"[41] he writes. That is, arrange the fuel where you are – know that you have to prepare for a long captivity, and it's easier to survive when you can have that piece of home and life to live.

Now, Jeremiah tells the people to "seek the *shalom*" of their exiled city. *Shalom* in Hebrew means both peace and wholeness – it's a wish that everything is "well with your soul," of being fully present to your situation. It's used as a greeting and a farewell and shows up everywhere in the Bible. To seek shalom means to try to make whole what is broken – to seek peace through wholeness instead of destruction. Here, in exile, that brokenness is especially felt – families separated by a 900-mile journey, the same distance as from Tulsa to Detroit, but made on foot! Not only that, but how do you have a community apart from the temple? Well, Jeremiah is saying to do exactly that: make a community where you are, even apart from the familiar rhythms that you were used to. That though the people are far away from home, God is in their midst, too – and they should seek to put things right that once went wrong. (And yes, that's basically the plot of Quantum Leap – a great example of seeking *shalom* no matter where – or when – you find yourself!)

You see, when we forgive others, we create sparks of *shalom*. When we reunite what has been broken, we rekindle the warm fire of *shalom*. And that is how we apply spiritual heat! In Luke 17, we see Jesus seeking the *shalom* of the outcast people in the town he happens to find himself in. Ten people with skin conditions – not leprosy as we know it today, but various skin conditions that might be equally as contagious – call out to Jesus in the distance. Jesus tells them to show themselves to the priests. Normally, that's what you do as the last step – to prove that you are no longer showing signs of the skin condition. But these people, pushed to the edges of their community, immediately do what Jesus tells them to do, and all are healed on their way. One of them, seeing his condition healed, returns to Jesus before doing what Jesus said to do! He's so overcome with gratitude that he has to come back immediately to thank Jesus. And Jesus praises him and lifts him up as an example. But here's the thing: the man who returned is a Samaritan, a group of people who were often ostracized by their distant relatives, the Jewish people – and likewise, ostracized the Jews as well. Jesus has provided *shalom* in healing the man's skin AND the man's standing. One who was low is brought high. The coals of community have been fanned into the warm campfire of *shalom*.

---

[41] Jeremiah 29: 4-7 (paraphrased)

The same spark that lit the campfires of the exiles, the disciples, and the tongues of flame of Pentecost is still with us today. Like the exiled people of Judah, we are called to arrange the fuel of our fire by living life as God calls us to – and apply heat to the community by seeking its *shalom*, continuing to lift each other up and fan the flames by praise and gratitude, to God and to each other. Then, God's light and warmth will truly be felt by all.

May you seek *shalom* for your community and the nation and the world. May the gifts of Christ Jesus fill you with healing words and deeds. May you always praise God and each other when the Spirit draws you to do good things.

Proclamation of the Word

Truth, Not Tricks
(Rev. Elana Levy)
Exodus 7:8-13; Isaiah 45:18-19; 2 Timothy 3:1-9

Every year, the *Oxford English Dictionary* picks a word of the year that their editorial staff feels, "reflect[s] the ethos, mood, or preoccupations of that particular year and [that will have] lasting potential as a word of cultural significance." Past years featured words like "selfie," "carbon footprint," "sudoku," and "unfriend." In 2016, the word they chose was, "post-truth" as in – we live in a post-truth era in which facts and evidence are increasingly seen as irrelevant. More important, we are told, is the truthiness of a thing – that the idea makes us feel like it is right because it appeals to us. Of course, no one can tell me that my feeling is wrong so attempts to discuss differing views become nothing more than meaningless strutting and peacocking.[42]

And beyond our culture's current insistence that the truth isn't real, all of us get sucked into the temptation to lie. In a study that was done in 2002, participants were engaged in ten-minute-long, everyday conversations. Would you believe me if I told you that 60% of the people lied 2-3 times? In ten minutes![43] And there wasn't even anything at stake!

Now, you don't have to read the Bible for too long before you realize that truth matters in scripture. The Lord tells Isaiah, "I the Lord speak the truth, I declare what is right." Jesus told us, "I am the way, the truth, and the life." And three times in the gospel of John, Jesus refers to the Holy Spirit as the, "Spirit of truth." Throughout scripture, we are told to beware of liars and deceivers and not to fall into the trap of becoming one ourselves. It's even in the Ten Commandments: do not bear false witness against your neighbor. Whether in formal settings or our private lives, scripture is clear that the truth is sacred, and it is part of our calling.

And that's where we meet Paul and Timothy in our epistle reading. Paul had spent several years in Ephesus growing the church and doing missionary work there. He knew the people at that church and he cared for them deeply,

---

[42] "Word of the Year," Oxford English Dictionary, accessed August 28.2018, https://en.oxforddictionaries.com/word-of-the-year.

[43] "UMass Amherst Researcher Finds Most People Lie in Everyday Conversation" UMass Amherst News & Media Relations, accessed August 28, 2018, https://www.umass.edu/newsoffice/article/umass-amherst-researcher-finds-most-people-lie-everyday-conversation

but God's calling doesn't always let us stay where our heart is. Paul left the church at Ephesus under the care of his friend and mission co-worker Timothy. In this letter, Paul is responding to reports of what's been going on in the church and trying to give Timothy some advice about how to proceed.

Since Paul has left Ephesus, other teachers have come in and the words they are preaching, and teaching are not truth. They are corrupted and counterfeit – not what Paul taught his brothers and sisters in Christ and not what Paul wants them to hear. He doesn't clarify exactly what their false teaching is – just that it isn't the truth. And the result of all of this deception is a catalogue of sins that would do the devil proud – selfishness, greediness, lack of self-control, abusiveness, brutality, treachery, recklessness, hedonism. Turning from truth, abandoning holiness is leading the people to turn from God, to turn from their communities and families, and heed only their own appetites.

Paul loves these Christians like they're his children and he needs them to see the light just as he did. And so, in very few words, he tells Timothy a Bible story. Remember when, my son, remember when Moses and Aaron were starting to lead the people of God? Moses had confronted pharaoh to, "let my people go," but pharaoh said, "I do not know your God." And so, Moses returned to challenge Pharaoh once more. But Pharaoh knew Moses, the Hebrew child who had grown up in his household. The Pharaoh was unimpressed by Moses' newfound identification with the people of his birth. "If you're so special – if I really should listen to you," Pharaoh said, "do a miracle for me." And just as the Lord told him to, Moses instructed Aaron to throw down his staff and turn it into a snake.

But Pharaoh was unimpressed and asked his magicians to do the same thing. And they cast spells and used their secret arts and they appeared to do the same thing. But, you know what? A trick is not the same thing as the truth. Aaron didn't need to cast spells to bind the serpent. The Lord commanded, and it happened. A miracle is when God gets involved beyond what humanity can do. Magic is when humanity mimics what only God can do.

That trick looked good enough to Pharaoh because Pharaoh was not interested in what was true. By the way, if you ever wondered, there is a way to do this trick that snake charmers have been practicing for many years. They can put strong pressure on a nerve just under the cobra's head and it get incredibly rigid. From a distance, it even looks like a staff. To finish the trick, the snake charmer throws it against the ground and the jolt sort of shakes the snake out of its catatonic state and it slithers on.[44] It's a good trick,

---

[44] Robert Jamieson, A.R. Fausset, and David Brown, *A Commentary on the Old and*

but it's still not the truth. That point is underscored because Aaron's staff swallows the magicians two staffs.

Ancient tradition called these two magicians Jannes and Jambres. They opposed Moses again and again, but Moses always showed them up because the word and the light of truth is beyond our preference, beyond our coaxing, and certainly beyond our control. And so, Paul reminds Timothy, just as the Egyptians could not enslave the people that God guaranteed would be free, so too would the false teachers in the early church be stopped. Opposing God is the greatest folly there is and the truth comes out eventually.

This is a great story. Paul ties the past and the present together so neatly and offers strong words of encouragement for young pastor Timothy. And I think it's a very appealing passage for us today as well. Look at these sinners – how awful they are! Avoid them. And think about all those silly women, so easily captivated by false teaching. Think of all those people, "who are always being instructed and can never arrive at a knowledge of the truth." We all know people like that, don't we? Well, thank God we aren't like *those* people!

And dear God, if there's any humility in us at all, this moment should give us pause. Because if we were those people, we probably wouldn't know it. And for each one we might point out, they'd probably say the same of us. So, the bigger question is not does the truth matter, we know that is does. The question becomes: how do we know the truth? If we take the challenge to seek the truth seriously, then the complexity can become mind numbing in a heartbeat.

But, fear not, God did not create the heavens and the earth to be a chaos. God did not tell us to seek the Lord in chaos. God speaks the truth and declares what is right. So, you might say, that simplifies things. We just open up the Bible and it will tell us what to do in every situation – argument over. This is, of course, why theology books are so short and understandable, yeah?

I'm sure you know what comes next – do I follow the passage of scripture that says act or the one that says to wait patiently on the Lord? Do I seek vengeance or offer forgiveness? Is it a time to build up or a time to break down? A time to seek, a time to lose? A time to keep, a time to throw away? A time to love, a time to hate? Ack! Our quest for truth needs more than an "open the Bible to a random page and do whatever that verse says" type theology.

New Testaments (Peabody: Hendrickson, 2002 reprint), 1:295.

The Bible itself teaches us how to tell what is true. Any teaching should pass three tests. First is the rule of love. Does this teaching reflect the love of God and Christ and Spirit? A love that created all that is, a love that gave his life for mine, a love that leads and protects me all the days of my life? Does it make me more loving and encourage others to be more loving?

Second is the rule of justice because our God is a God of justice who seeks the well-being of all: great or small, rich or poor, old or young. Does this teaching lead to greater justice and equality in the world? Is it concerned with fairness and human dignity? Does it lift up others and show them to be cherished children of God?

Third and lastly is the rule of faith. Does this teaching emerge from scripture and the traditions of the church? Does it reflect trust in God as our help and the source of our life? Can it stand up to scrutiny within the community of Christ?[45]

My friends, truth comes from God and it cannot be contained by us. Neither can we ever grasp it fully. And that is why we are called to be humble in community. That is why we are called to seek the truth and to speak what we have found AND to listen to one another. As we test the teachings, we must ask ourselves, does it pass the rule of love? Does it pass the rule of justice? Does it pass the rule of faith? In hope and prayer, we trust that the Spirit helps us discern this light – to truly be the church reformed, always reforming. The Spirit can give us eyes to see and ears to hear a new word of truth if we open our hearts to it. May we seek the light of truth each day of our lives. Amen.

---

[45] Thanks to Dr. Tyler Mayfield for this rubric, discussed in his "Ethics of Violence in the Old Testament Class," 2013.

Voice at the Gate
(Rev. Lucus Keppel)
John 10:1-10, 14-16; Isaiah 43:1-7

A few years ago, when I was living in the village of Corona in New Mexico, I came home from a long trip to find that my across-the-street neighbor had bought three lambs from the state fair. These lambs were incredibly cute and cuddly – with their big eyes and short little bodies, they looked like cartoon animals brought to life. But they were clearly not used to living in a small pen – they ran from one side to the other, bleating constantly. Now, my office had a window that faced the sheep, and though their bleating was cute at first, it gradually drove me to distraction. So, I decided to try something – I walked outside of the house, faced the sheep-pen at my neighbors – and said "maa-aaa" in my finest imitation of their bleats. Immediately, they settled down – stopped bleating, and one that had been walking from one side of the pen to the other lay down on the ground. Satisfied, I walked back into the house – and then got to thinking: *What does "maa-aaa" mean in Sheep-tongue?*

Perhaps I was thinking of the old joke about cats and dogs – most of us end up imitating their voices at one point of another, saying "woof!" to dogs and "mew" to cats. Well, if we could understand their responses, the dogs would be saying, "Hey! You speak Dog? That's great! I have no idea what you said, but good try! Here, let me teach you – woof, woof!"

Meanwhile, the cats would be saying, in their slow languid way: "Oh, are you trying to speak Cat? What you said makes no sense, so until you get it exactly right, I'm going to ignore you."

I'm still not entirely sure what I actually said to the lambs, but I'm glad they seemed to give me credit for trying. I didn't get to improve my sheep-tongue, as the lambs soon were sent out to the ranch, where they had lots of room to wander about and eat the grass of the high plains. I did get to visit another sheep-ranch, though, and learned that even today, sheep come back to a protected area to sleep, no matter how far they've wandered during the day. If they get lost, they listen for the calls of their fellow sheep – and especially the voice of their shepherd. Even if there are multiple herds of sheep grazing on common land, the sheep know their shepherd's voice, and will come to their shepherd alone.

In John's Gospel, we see this same idea at work. Many villages in Galilee and Judea had communal sheep-folds, where the sheep owned by many families would shelter together. That way, one family at a time could watch over them, instead of every family having to keep watch constantly. Now, if you owned sheep, and wanted to take them out of the fold to graze, you would turn up at the gate, and the family watching the sheep that day would let you call out to your sheep to follow you to the trails. If you didn't go to the gate, instead climbing over a fence, and grabbing a lamb, it was pretty clear that you weren't the owner of the lamb. In John, Jesus uses this example to show what it means to be the true shepherd. A true shepherd doesn't use violence, doesn't sneak in, doesn't steal the sheep away. No – a true shepherd calls the sheep by name, and they know the shepherd and follow where the shepherd leads.

But, this story wasn't understood – so Jesus tries to make it more plain: He says,

> *I assure you, I am the gate for the sheep… whoever enters through me will be saved. They will be able to come in and go out. They will find everything they need. A thief comes to steal, kill, and destroy – but I came to give life – life that is full and good.*[46]

All well and good – but why, in trying to clarify, does Jesus say, "I am the gate." That's – confusing, at best, to us today. But take a look at this picture:[47]

---

[46] John 10:7-10 (CEB/Barclay)

[47] Shepherd at the Gate, Nazareth Village, Israel. Personal photograph by Lucus Keppel, January 2011.

Note the shepherd standing at the entry to the sheepfold. Folds like this would be used when the sheep couldn't make it back to the village at night. Notice that there's no door, or gate to the fold – it's an opening that's fairly wide, but still small enough for a person laying down to block it completely. And that's exactly what shepherds at folds like these would do – the shepherd becomes the gate, keeping the sheep inside.

When Jesus says: "I am the Gate", he's claiming to be the shepherd – and will directly state so a few chapters later. And unlike my futile attempts to speak lamb-tongue, Jesus not only speaks our language, but calls each of us by name. Now, names have a certain power in today's world – we sign our name to contracts big and small as a symbol of honor. We also tend to look up, or answer, if someone says a name that's even a little like ours – which causes confusion and giggles in coffeeshops and classrooms alike. In the ancient world, names were believed to possess power over a person. It was believed that a child's name shaped their destiny – and that if you knew someone's true name, you would have power over them. That's what's going on in the Rumplestiltskin fairy-tale – knowing his true name gave the young woman power over him. People would take particular pains to hide their true names, going by nicknames except with close family. But listen to what God says through the Prophet Isaiah: "Fear not; I have redeemed you. I have called you by name – you are mine!"[48] God calls us by name, claiming ultimate power over us – and tells us not to fear, because God has claimed us. God has priority. Now, if God were vengeful, terrible, or tyrannical, that would be a scary statement. But God is love – and God's claim of us is a claim of grace, of freedom, and love. Jesus reminds us that the sheep are free to go in and come out – that they have freedom of motion, can seek the fold when needing shelter, and can seek food when hungry. The True Shepherd cares for the flock, leading them to new pastures and into safety when needed.

That God calls us by our true name is vitally important. You see, the Jewish people were intimately familiar with being re-named by their conquerors – and nowhere is this more clear than in the story of Daniel and his friends, Hannaniah, Mishael, and Azariah. Their names have specific meanings in Hebrew – Daniel means "God is my Judge," while the other three mean "Adonai is Gracious" "Who is like God?" and "Adonai Helps", respectively. When they were carried to Babylon after the fall of Jerusalem, you may remember from the "Testing God" chapter that they were all renamed: Balthazzar, Shadrach, Meshach, and Abednego. Their names, their identities, were changed to fit the language of their oppressors – but they remembered

---

[48] Isaiah 43:1b

that God called them by their true names, and were not afraid, even in the midst of those who were trying to harm them.

Sadly, we Americans have acted more like the Babylonians from this story than the Hebrew people. In encountering native people, not only did we force different names on them – either changing syllables to something quote "more pronounceable" – like Hiawatha from Haio-went-ha, or turning the Chavez into Jarvis – or just assigning a new name altogether, like was done routinely on plantations and in native boarding schools. My friends, take care to learn someone's name – as they would have you say it – and you'll go far in showing the same love and respect for people that God does.

Not every contact between native peoples and Europeans led to this level of disrespect and, ultimately, violence. Think of how differently things would be if we took Jesus' reminder that there are sheep in folds different from ours more seriously! For instance, let me tell you the story of Rev. Egerton Young, who was a Methodist minister and missionary in 19th century Saskatchewan, Canada.

As a young minister, riding circuit between far-flung churches, he befriended a fellow minister who was of the Cree peoples, and learned their Algonquin dialect. Rev. Young and his wife went to live in a lodge with several families of the Cree who had never heard the Gospel stories and proceeded to teach the message of God's love for the world. After Rev. Young finished with a prayer, one of the elders said, "When you spoke of the Great Spirit just now, did I hear you say, "Our Father"? This is very new and sweet to me. We never thought of the great Spirit as Father. We heard him in the thunder; we saw him in the lightening, the tempest, and the blizzard, and we were afraid. So when you tell us that the great Spirit is our Father, that is very beautiful to us." After a moment, he went on to ask, "Missionary, did you say that the Great Spirit is *your* Father?" Of course, Rev. Young answered, "Yes!" "And did you also say that the Great Spirit is Father of the Cree?" "I did!" "Then, we are brothers!"[49]

Truly, we are all children of God – and God calls us by name. Soon after God says, "I have called you by name – you are mine" in Isaiah, God says "…everyone is called by my name…." In other words, God calls us – all of us – by name – and that name belongs to God. God is the true shepherd, the one who knows your name, calls your name, and leads you in and out of the fold. When you feel lost, listen for the voice of the shepherd, calling your

---

[49] William Barclay, "The Ultimate Unity," in *The Gospel of John*, Revised ed. Vol. 2, The Daily Study Bible Series, (Philadelphia: Westminster Press, 1975), 62-63.

name. It might sound like your voice – it might sound like the voice of your mother or father – it might sound like the voice of your truelove or your child. Any which way, you'll know it by its loving sound. It is the True Shepherd that leads us out and back in, that keeps us safe, that guides our way. And it is the True Shepherd that is the voice not only at the gate of our fold, but the gate of our neighbor, and the gate of our siblings across the whole planet.

May you hear the voice of the Shepherd and may you follow the way the Shepherd leads. May God call you by name, and may you love God so much that names fall away and you are just constantly in the company of God – our Father, the Shepherd, and the Spirit. Amen!

Affirmation of Faith

A Vulnerable Embrace
(Rev. Elana Levy)
Luke 2:1-20

As I read and re-read the Christmas story in Luke this year, I couldn't help but notice how it speaks of power. It begins with a decree from the Emperor to register the people. It goes on to speak of the governor, the next most powerful man in the lives of the chosen people. The governor would orchestrate the census and the taxing. Then, we meet Joseph and Mary. By all accounts, they're nobody special – just two regular people among millions in the empire. They aren't Roman citizens so they don't have too many rights. They aren't allowed to vote and if a Roman citizen attacks them, the courts won't hear their case. A Roman official could come to their town and draft as many soldiers as they please and take extra taxes to fund wars that are of no benefit to the conquered people. Those who resisted are beaten, jailed, killed. Joseph and Mary keep their heads down and do as they're told.[50]

In most any historical telling, the poor couple expecting their first child is not frontpage news. It's emperors and kings and governors who move mountains and reshape the world according to their design. But this is our story – our new beginning that challenges us to look at the world and then look again. Now, we know that Mary and Joseph are not totally in the dark here. Angels told both of them about this miraculous pregnancy, the coming of the Son of God, as the angel Gabriel told Mary. But that doesn't mean that their journey is easy. It doesn't mean that they aren't scared.

Because beyond the empire's political machinations, beyond the three-days' journey to an ancestral home, beyond the swollen feet, heartburn, retained water, insomnia, constant cravings, and exhaustion of late pregnancy, Mary and Joseph are very much alone. Back home in Nazareth, Mary's surprise pre-marital pregnancy would've been a great scandal – a naughty girl and the poor chump who's marrying her anyway. How many of her friends would've hung in there with her despite the gossip and rumors? How many of her soon to be in-laws would've stopped giving her the side eye long enough to really get to know her? And then, as they travel to Bethlehem, everywhere they go is filled with strangers. In hard times, that can feel even lonelier than being alone.

---

[50] "Roman Citizenship," in *Wikipedia: The Free Encyclopedia*, Wikimedia Foundation Inc., updated 27 August 2018, https://en.wikipedia.org/wiki/Roman_citizenship.

When the time came to give birth, her mother wasn't there – not any sisters or cousins or aunts or friends. Hopefully, someone fetched the local midwife to help. But, really, that moment could've been just Mary and Jesus, bringing forth new life together – in moments both painful and glorious; strained and beautiful. And as she first held him and wrapped him in bands of cloth, we can be sure that there was a most vulnerable embrace.

This word – vulnerable – I think it fits the moment perfectly. Because you might hear the word and think of someone who is exposed, helpless, powerless. You might think of someone who could be harmed at any moment. And we find out in Matthew 2 how much danger they are truly in when Herod orders his massacre and the Holy Family must flee. Being unsafe is part of the story, but it's not the whole story. When we look at our most intimate relationships, we also speak of vulnerability. And here, it means a willingness to be open to the one that you love. It means letting your guard down, trusting them, showing up for them even if you might get hurt. This vulnerability is rare and special. It is to be reserved for only the few who show themselves worthy of such closeness.

When I was quite little – maybe 3 years old – I was riding on the highway with my Mom and the car broke down. Now, I'm in my thirties. I may be young, but back when I was 3, nobody had cell phones. It was just you and your vehicle waiting on a Good Samaritan while hundreds of cars whizzed past without giving you a second look. Being 3, I don't think I really understood the situation, but I remember that Mom seemed frustrated and worried. I was more interested in whatever toy I had brought along for the ride. Then, before too long, a car pulled over. It had a Jesus fish on the bumper. The people spoke to my Mom and offered to help get her to a gas station pay phone and she agreed. As I crawled in after her, I gleefully thought, "How wonderful that my Mom just so happens to know these nice, helpful people so that we can get moving! How lucky is that that they drove past at just this very moment!" And I went back to my toy. I am, perhaps, a little embarrassed to admit that I didn't rethink that assessment of the situation until I was in high school – not because I figured it out, but because I randomly asked Mom about it. "Of course, I didn't know them," she said. "I was scared to get into the car with you there, but I thought maybe the Jesus fish meant that we'd be okay."

It had never occurred to me that we weren't safe and that Mom took a risk. But suddenly, the whole event changed in my mind. We were stranded, helpless, vulnerable and Mom took a chance on the kindness of strangers. And the people that picked us up took a chance that the woman with a child wasn't – I dunno – hiding a gun in her purse to steal their car and their wallets.

If you've met my mother, you'll know how absurd that would be, but still... In offering to help us, they, too, were vulnerable. We all could've gotten hurt, but, instead, that shared vulnerability helped us all move forward.

Let's face it, at no time in our lives are we as vulnerable than when we are babies and children. Our lives are literally in our parents' hands, in the hands of the ones who raise us. If we are lucky, we never question that safety and love and security like three-year-old me on the side of the road. So, as we return to our Gospel lesson, we can see that it wasn't just Mary and Joseph and the shepherds and conquered peoples who were vulnerable on that day. Jesus was, too – tiny and fragile, unable to speak and totally dependent on his mother and father. God chose to be vulnerable to us in the most striking possible way. In Jesus Christ, even from the moment of his birth, we learn that God is not so distant as we sometimes fear. Jesus chose to be so close to us that we could shake his hand or strike his cheek; we could anoint his feet or take his life. And in this moment of birth, we see a God in baby Jesus who loves us so much that he is there for us even though we sometimes cause him pain.

The choices that we make – the lives that we lead affect God and always have. But this God never stops showing up for us. One of the miracles of the incarnation is that it teaches us that God believed in Mary so much that God came to her as a little baby. Despite every sinful thing that she might have done or would yet do, God believed in her and became vulnerable to her and trusted her. During the Christmas season, as you prepare for whatever festivities you have planned for today or tomorrow, I want you to consider that whatever the state of your faith or the mistakes you might make, God believes in you – God believes in all of us. We are all part of that vulnerable embrace. And so, lean into those everlasting arms, let them strengthen you and gladden your heart. Join the shepherds in glorifying and praising God and let your life be changed because the God that believes in you can do miraculous things through you, too. Amen.

The God Who Gave You Birth
(Rev. Elana Levy)
*Proverbs 6:20-23; Deuteronomy 32:1-3, 10-13, 15b-18;
John 2:1-12*

Growing up, I would see my extended family for the major holidays. I remember one Easter visit to my grandparents in Maryland. There were seven of us grandkids, so our parents regularly shuttled us out of the house to tire us out. That day, they took the lot of us to a park. Now, I must have been about middle school aged at the time and I have a cousin who's 6 years younger than me. As soon as we arrived at the park, we were all getting out of the cars and he shut his finger in the car door. I think I was the only one who saw him do it and I thought, "oh, crap. This is gonna be bad." But his face was blank, in total shock. I asked him, "Chris, are you okay?" And he didn't say a word. He just wandered around, searching seriously, earnestly, until he found his mother. Then, holding his finger in front of him, he started wailing and crying, falling into her open arms. The moment struck me and, if I'm being totally honest, it confused me to no end. What was with the time delay? Didn't it hurt when it first happened? How on earth did finding his Mom mean that pain would suddenly be expressed – and loudly?

Maybe you have a similar story. There's something about finding that one who soothes and nurtures and tries to make all the pain go away that opens us up to let the pain out and to let it go. Having that person to go to – being that person for someone else – it is truly a sacred and beautiful thing. But I'm not going to stand here this morning and pretend that we all experience motherhood the same way. Some of us were blessed with rich, full, beautiful experiences of motherhood: as children, as mothers ourselves. But others have wounds from childhood; others struggled to have children or experienced motherhood as loss, grief, and conflict. Still others did not feel the calling to be mothers. For those of you who might be wary of a sermon about mothers, it's not about measuring up: you must be this good at mothering to be blessed by God. Neither is it a rod of judgment, holding up an impossible standard to accuse and dismiss the hard work of giving life and nurturing it. This morning, we will be looking at mothering as part of the divine image: something that embraces both our love and our lack of love; our victories and our struggles.

You'll have to forgive me – this sermon will proceed like Russian nesting dolls: within each mothering image, there is another smaller mother image, and on and on. So, we begin with creation. Before there was us, there was a

Trinitarian God, one being in infinite relationship: Father, Son, Holy Spirit. More than any other single word, this God can be defined as love: overflowing, outpouring, and endless. And this God of love created all that is so that all creation would know the beauty of love and life. When humans were created in the image of God, this creative impulse to make life and love flourish was one of our earliest gifts. After all, the first ever commandment in the Bible is, "be fruitful and multiply." Here, God invites us to be partners in creation – to feel what it means to create, to give new life, in a sense, to mother whether we have children or not.

This theme carries forward in scripture to the first mother, Eve. Her name itself is related to the word for "life." Adam calls her the, "mother of all living." And Eve understands her connection to life itself very intimately. Yes, I know she was tempted and they both sinned. Yes, she and Adam were summarily booted from the garden, but… she remembers God when she gives birth to her firstborn. She calls him Cain, which is related to the verb that means, "to get," "to acquire." She names him "Cain" because, as she says in Genesis 4: "I have gotten a man from the Lord." Eve sees that she has created something new together with God and so she, and not Adam, names this new creature; and she is overwhelmed with awe and praise.

So, this God who mothered all creation into existence has also gifted humanity with the ability to mother and bring forth new life, but there are yet more nesting dolls. We move ahead through Abraham to find that God has called a people into being: where there were no people, now there is a people of God. Where only idols and falsehoods were known, now there is revelation of beauty and truth. The passage from Deuteronomy comes from one of the many speeches of Moses near the end of his life. The people are almost there – almost across the border into the promised land – but Moses knows that he won't be joining them. So, he preaches many sermons and makes many speeches to remind them of who God is, who they are, and how they should respond.

What's interesting about the images that he chooses, though, is that most of them are about God mothering the people. Moses compares God to a mother eagle who protects her young and teaches them how to fly. Moses talks about God shielding, caring, and guarding the people – even feeding and nursing them so that they would grow strong and healthy. And since God has been closer and more sustaining than any human mother could possibly be, Moses is shocked and dismayed that the people have gone after foreign Gods. The verse that closes this section is pointed, indeed: "You were unmindful of the Rock that bore you; you forgot the God who gave you birth." In this verse, we find Hebrew poetry with the two lines in parallel. It's difficult to tell from our translation, but, "the Rock that bore you" is closer to "begot"- the word that would be used for a father of a child. Coupled together with the next line, "the God who gave you birth," we see that Moses is saying that this God, your God, is father and mother to you. For all the good and the bad you experience in life otherwise, you always have God as father and mother, unfailing and constant.

I love this line, "the God who gave you birth" and it percolates around my mind. And out of the blue, it struck me: this God who gave us birth was also born. I don't mean in the beginning, before all creation, but as a little baby: Jesus of Nazareth. This means that not only do we have a God at whose command life exploded onto the watery deep, a God who showed us the joy of nurturing new life, a God who created and called together a holy people; our God has personally experienced motherhood from both sides. When Jesus came to earth, he decided to be mothered by his own broken creation – to be vulnerable, to have the ancient equivalent of a diaper change, to have boo boos and scars, to grow under human guidance. God showed us the blessing of receiving and accepting love and nurture just as surely as we are blessed to give love and nurture.

And we don't have terribly many stories of Jesus relating to his earthly mother, but the wedding in Cana is surely a crowd pleaser. In the Gospel of John, there are only two prominent stories of Jesus and Mary: Jesus changing water into wine at the beginning of his public ministry and Mary at the foot of the cross at the end of Jesus' life. Here, Jesus and his disciples have been invited to a wedding. It seems likely that it was for a family friend or a relative. After all, Mary is keeping better tabs on the wine supply than even the servants and the chief steward. Mary seems to be the first one to notice that the wine is out, and she tells Jesus. Jesus seems to demur, but Mary tells the servants that they should do whatever Jesus says to do: a recipe for excitement if ever I heard one. Now, the stone water jars were there for hand washing – they were at a feast, after all – and in total they would hold 120-180 gallons of water. That much water would weigh at least 200 pounds (and that's not counting the weight of the jars!).[51] Jesus just says fill them up and let the chief steward taste some.

Now, even though this is the first act of Jesus' public ministry in John, there's something quite interesting about it. It's public and private at the same time. Think about it: who knows about this miracle? Mary, Jesus, and the servants.

---

[51] Bob Deffinbaugh, "5. The First Sign: Jesus Turns Water into Wine (John 2:1-11)," Bible.org, August 19, 2004, https://bible.org/seriespage/5-first-sign-jesus-turns-water-wine-john-21-11

All the chief steward knows is that the wine is good and he commends the, almost certainly very confused, bridegroom. The guests don't know, the family doesn't know – just those who listened to Jesus and trusted his word.

Jesus listened to his mother and he saved the wedding celebration. At that time, to run out of supplies for a wedding feast would have been a great shame and dishonor to a family. But there is Jesus, hearing his mother's request, tending to human concern, and providing with impossible abundance beyond what one would ever ask. Like so many mothers, he works behind the scenes – not for the credit, not for attention, but for the good of the family. As the unnamed married couple start their new life, Jesus starts his and heads out into the world.

In Eastertide, we remember that Jesus lived and died and was reborn – appearing in many places and to many different people. God raised Jesus to new life. In Christ, this mothering impulse to love and give life does not cease. It rings through all of our lives, our new families, our deaths, and our rebirth. So, to worship our mothering God, to honor the mothering souls in all our lives, let us give life and nurture and cherish it wherever we find it on the path before us. If it be through children, let us love and raise them with all our hearts. If it be through creative endeavor: through art and design and construction, let us create for the flourishing of all. If it be through justice and service work, let us proudly work with and on behalf of the least among us as the saints before have taught us. Whatever you do, remember the soul of the small child seeking comfort and relief – and remember God works through those with soothing words and strengthens our every step. Amen.

Offering and Stewardship

The Joy of... Work?!
(Rev. Elana Levy)
Ecclesiastes 3:9-15; Isaiah 65:17-19, 21-25

The summer after my Junior year of college, I was a counselor at a Girl Scout camp outside Williamsburg, Virginia. Given my great maturity and advanced age of 20 whole years old, they made me a unit leader – directly responsible for 25-30 girls who were 9-11 years old with maybe 2 counselors working under me who were around 16 years old. This meant keeping track of the paperwork, being the ultimate resolver of sometimes endless disputes, and being responsible for the epi-pen (while praying it would never be needed). When I say "camp," I mean that we actually camped in tents, outside in the heat, humidity, and mosquito swarms that rival most any part of the country. We did eat most of our meals in a, mercifully, air-conditioned dining hall except for one night of every week when we would cook out at a campfire at our own campsites.

The girls usually loved that night. Each of them had jobs mixing, chopping, preparing their meals, getting the fire ready, eagerly awaiting dessert. This went off without a hitch every week – every week except one when the sky was just a shade grayer than we'd hoped. Not to be deterred, I and the other counselors urged the girls to keep chopping – keep prepping – even as the rain began to come down. It started slowly at first, giving me ample room to hold out hope for our special treat, but before too long it was pouring down. One by one, the girls and the other counselors retreated to our shelter to wait out the storm.

I don't know why, but I refused to give up on our campfire meal. No matter how much it rained, I was determined to feed my girls – to follow through and do whatever it took to get them what they needed. As it happened, the dinner menu for that evening called for a cherry cobbler made in a Dutch oven – an enormous cast iron pot. This pot covered enough of the fire that I could slide the foil dinners the girls had made underneath it and cook them over the sheltered flame and the coals. So there I was, soaking wet, turning over the dinners while 30ish girls looked at me like I was nuts. Before too long, the meals were cooked. I got them out of the fire and we ate together.

Just as we started to eat, the Assistant Camp Director came by in a golf cart offering us peanut butter and jelly sandwiches for dinner. "We don't need that!" I proclaimed proudly, dripping on the ground. No other campsite had been able to finish their dinner – just us.

That was a really good day at work. I was beaming, I felt powerful – I provided for my people when no one else could. But, if I'm being totally honest, I can hear Qoheleth[52] looking over my shoulder and laughing, "Vanity of vanities! All is vanity. What do people gain from all the hard work that they work so hard at under the sun?" I busted my tail, got filthy from tending the fire, was smeared with ash and sweat and rain…and after all that, the Assistant Camp Director was bringing food anyway. Did that work really matter? Does anyone else even remember it except crazy, weirdly proud me? Did it matter at all?

We don't usually talk about work at church. If we do, we tend to talk more about vocation and calling, about the works of service that are part and parcel of the Christian life. But our jobs are a huge part of our lives. We spend, on average, 90,000 hours at work over our lifetimes.[53] And, according to a study from 2010, 80% of people are dissatisfied with their jobs – 80%![54] In another survey that came out in 2016, only 6% of the adults polled said that they had achieved their dream job.[55]

Work takes up a huge portion of our lives, our identities, so I think Qoheleth's question is important for us still today, "What do workers gain from all their hard work?" As we read Ecclesiastes, we follow the moral, spiritual, philosophical journey of one who is called Qoheleth. "Qoheleth" means a "person who speaks before the assembly," which is often shortened to "Preacher" or "Teacher" in English. Qoheleth has seen people working themselves to the bone. Qoheleth has, it seems, indulged in every pleasure, built buildings, planted vineyards, chased after wisdom, each time wondering – did any of it matter?

The passage we have from Ecclesiastes this morning is a response of faith to that question of meaninglessness. It comes right after the much more often

---

[52] Qoheleth – pronounced "ko-Hell-ett"

[53] Jenna Goudreau, "Find Happiness at Work," *Forbes*, March 4, 2010, https://www.forbes.com/2010/03/04/happiness-work-resilience-forbes-woman-well-being-satisfaction.html

[54] Alyson Shontell, "80% Hate Their Jobs – But Should You Choose a Passion or a Paycheck?" *Business Insider*, October 4, 2010, https://www.businessinsider.com/what-do-you-do-when-you-hate-your-job-2010-10

[55] Sam Greenspan, "83 Percent of Adults Are Still Trying to Get Their Dream Job (See the 11 We Still Want)," *11 Points*, August 4, 2016, http://11points.com/83-percent-adults-still-trying-get-dream-job-see-11-still-want/

cited verses, "For everything there is a season and a time to every purpose under heaven." Having considered all of this, Qoheleth marvels that, "everything is beautiful in its time, but [God] has also placed eternity in [our] hearts." We work hard, we succeed, we fail, we dream of better lives, better days, better work – but through it all, God has placed eternity in our hearts. And we don't get to know how it all began and how it will end, but God does. And that means that our work can carry a hope of impact and purpose, our failures and missteps will not destroy the possibility of goodness moving forward. Whatever God does lasts forever and as we live and as we work, we are a part of what God does.

And so, Qoheleth tells us, "I know that there's nothing better for [workers] than to enjoy themselves and do what's good while they live. This is the gift of God: that all people should eat, drink, and enjoy the results of their hard work." "Enjoy yourself" is not a message we're used to hearing from scripture (or, I suppose, in many churches). Enjoy yourself and do what's good. This includes work, too! Qoheleth encourages us to look for joy in the work that we're doing, to see that work is connected to the gift of God and to our communities and our world. In the ancient world, they didn't have as many choices: the work of the farm, the garden, the metal worker, the mason, the chef. They apprenticed and usually worked within the household or at a particular trade. We have more choice in what we do and the way we fill our days. Our work, paid and unpaid, can feed our spirit, too, and remind us of God's glory.

As I mentioned earlier, many are in jobs they don't like. Most of us have had jobs that just felt like torture. So we look forward to rest, vacation, retirement. But according to the Bible, we were made to work. In Genesis 2, when God creates the world and then creates Adam, scripture says that God, "put him in the garden of Eden to till it and keep it." Adam – the world's first professional gardener.

In our Isaiah passage, we hear a prophecy about God creating new heavens and a new earth – a phrase that puts us in mind of the kingdom of heaven come to earth, the final restoration, the paradise of heaven. Isaiah 65 is a beautiful vision of peace, joy, gladness, and rejoicing. But it has some unexpected details – it says that the people will build houses and inhabit them, plant vineyards and eat their fruit. It says that we shall, "long enjoy the work of [our] hands." As far as descriptions of heaven go, this is a far cry from sleepy saints, dressed in white, floating by on cloud-shaped La-z-boys, harp in hand. In this paradise even the wolf and the lamb go out to eat together (and they both make it home safe!). Isaiah tells us that in heaven we will work, too. But there won't be an impatient, unpleasable, yelling boss.

There won't be drought and famine and small critters nibbling away at the fields. There won't be wars and hatred and violence. The vision of heaven that Isaiah has received is one where we take on the projects that we love without our health and energy slowing us down. This vision is one where we can build and enjoy, create and marvel, explore and uncover without fear of danger or things coming unraveled before our eyes.

On a long enough timeline, it's hard for most of us to sit still, to be unengaged. It's hard for most of us to run up against earthly limitations that restrict the ways we can follow what we are passionate about. Qoheleth wondered: Does our work matter? The Lord answers every time, "yes!" Who we are, what we love, what we can imagine does not come to nothing. Indeed, it's one of the ways we are made in God's image, part of God's own creative spark. So, keep your campfire burning in the rain, know that your gifts and efforts are blessed by God, and share what you've been given wherever you can, knowing that heaven will be full of life. Amen.

Mary Speaks and Bartholomew Speaks
(Revs. Levy & Keppel)
John 12: 1-11; John 13 (Selected verses)

In this dialogue sermon, we each chose a character from the Maundy Thursday[56] lectionary readings and presented our character's view of events. It was only after writing the two halves of the sermon that we merged them and added the intercut dialogue. While delivering the sermon on Maundy Thursday, we wore simple Bible-era tunics to add to the dramatic nature of the sermon.

Bartholomew:

Hi, Mary! Peace be with you.

Mary:

And also with you. Things are so tense in Jerusalem these days. The cheerful cries of last Sunday seemed to vanish just as suddenly as they began. I'm glad I ran into you, Bartholomew, I've been looking for one of the twelve. I've been so worried about Jesus since he left my house.

Bartholomew:

Yeah, I haven't seen you since you anointed Jesus' feet. What happened that night?"

Mary:

Well, you know, at first the evening was going so well. Everyone's cup over-flowed and no one's plate was empty. It was a chorus of clanking plates and lips smacking in delight. Then, the noshing gave way to conversation – big laughs, glowing cheeks, warm smiles. I stayed at the table and Martha was so happy she didn't even fuss at me. I just ate and soaked it all in.

---

[56] Maundy Thursday is the Thursday of Holy Week, three days before Easter Sunday. It marks the last supper with the disciples and Judas' betrayal of Jesus into the hands of the officials. The name comes from the Latin *Maundatum* or commandment, since on that night in the Gospel of John, Jesus gives a command to the disciples to love one another as Jesus loved them.

And, I guess the eating and talking went on, but I didn't notice it as much anymore. Night had fallen, and a cool breeze curled around the corner of the window pane. It raised goosebumps on my neck. I looked up and I caught Jesus' eyes. His eyes were always so full of life – like he knew everything there was to know about you, about everything. Looking into his eyes, I usually felt challenged and loved all at once. But his usual twinkle wasn't there. All of a sudden, he wasn't celebrating either. He had one of those, "now my soul is troubled" kind of looks.

Bartholomew:

I didn't notice that at all. It seemed like such an upbeat night. I wonder: what could trouble Jesus?

Mary:

No one else seemed to notice either. You guys didn't seem to see this sadness choking him from the inside. He was suffering alone, but surrounded by all the people who should have known him best – people who should have seen that anguish. I honestly don't know what came over me. I remember thinking that I wanted more than anything for him to be able to enjoy this celebration in honor of the miracle he performed that touched my heart so dearly.

And then ringing through my head, I heard these words from Isaiah 52, "How beautiful upon the mountains are the feet of the one who brings good news, who proclaims peace, who proclaims salvation, who says to Zion, 'Your God reigns.'" How beautiful he was, yet how sad, how – well – lonely. Before I even knew what I was doing, I had rushed to the other room and back with the costly perfume in hand. You all stopped eating. My brother Lazarus looked at me in shocked silence and I could feel my sister's scowl from the other room. But it didn't matter – it didn't matter. My friend, my brother, my Lord had sorrow, and I wanted to soothe him. I poured out that perfume on his blessed, beautiful feet. I couldn't speak – I didn't have words. But I wanted him to know, to feel in his flesh that he was loved – that we did care for him; that we were grateful; that at least one person recognized his sorrow. I couldn't make it any better. All I could do was love him with everything I had.

He was speechless – we were all speechless. The perfume pooled on the floor. I took down my hair to sop it up. I wiped his feet with my hair and then, for the first time since I got up, I looked up at him. It was like we were the only two people in the room. He saw my gift of love – my immense desire to ease his pain – and he looked like his heart would burst. The tears streamed down my cheeks, the smell of the perfume filled the house, it seemed to overcome everyone's senses. For a moment I thought that everyone was sharing this moment. But then, Judas spoke. "Why was this perfume not sold for three hundred denarii and the money given to the poor?"

I thought my heart would break right then and there. Maybe I had been wrong; maybe it was wasteful; maybe Jesus didn't see what I meant to show him. My face reddened, and I slumped over. But Jesus looked him square in the eye and said, "Leave her alone. She bought it so that she might keep it for the day of my burial."

So that was it – that was where the sorrow came from. Jesus was going to die. And I could see from the way he spoke that this is what he meant to do. I don't want him to die. I don't want to lose him. See, you and I know that he's – he's not just another teacher. There's something more about him. What man can raise someone from the dead? Who can walk on water and feed multitudes? Who can bring such peace and good news to those who follow him? When Jesus raised Lazarus from the dead, Martha and I saw the Messiah. My Lord and my God, he is.

He's finally come, and he ate in my house and he taught with authority, truth, and beauty. He is the One. And if he is to die, I will try to be brave. If he raised up my brother – who knows what he can do now.

Bartholomew:

All this time, Jesus has been teaching us with authority and doing miracles and being filled with God's power. Every day I work to understand even a little bit of what he's been teaching. It's hard to think that he might leave us. Do you remember what he said to you that night? "You always have the poor with you, but you do not always have me?" What do you think he meant by that?

Mary:

Well, just the other day Martha and Lazarus and I were talking about this passage from Deuteronomy 15, "…there will never cease to be poor in the land. Therefore, I command you, 'You shall open wide your hand to your brother and sister, to the needy and to the poor, in your land.'" God has charged us with taking care of the poor with hands that share our bounty, our love, our very selves – and here was Jesus saying the same thing. That night, Jesus was as the poor, the outcast, and the needy so I covered him with all the love in my heart. And his words inscribed themselves within me – today you serve me, a living body before you; tomorrow you serve others. Tomorrow you transform that love that you feel for me into healing touch and hearty meals and kind words, showing the love and dignity that you showed me today.

Jesus told me, told all of us that love is the best response even when it doesn't make sense. And when he left the next morning, Jesus continued to walk that path of love. And, yes, I believe him when he said that that path will lead to his death. My outpouring of love didn't save him. He's setting out to do something much greater for all of us.

Bartholomew:

Mary, you and I both know that Jesus has been talking about going to his death for a while now, but especially this week. Peter even challenged him on it – told him that surely, he wouldn't die, and Jesus rebuked him. I know some of the guys have been talking about Jesus like he's gonna swoop in and conquer Rome – or at least throw them out of Jerusalem. But tonight – tonight Jesus surprised us all again.

Mary:

Where is he? I'd like to see him.

Bartholomew:

He was here for a long while, but he took Peter, James, and John into the olive grove to pray. Before that, though – before that, Mary, he did something that turned everything upside down. We were already seated at the table when Jesus got back up and just started washing our feet without saying anything.

Mary:

The Lord of all was washing your feet? Like a servant?! I don't believe it!

Bartholomew:

No, really– he made a big deal of it, grabbed a basin and filled it with water from the jar at the door, and went to us, one by one. We were sitting down already, reclining on the cushions, and he took our feet – covered with dust and grime – he took our *feet*, and washed them, cleaned them. He cared for us like a servant does. And then, he wiped our feet clean with a towel. One by one, each of us, in the most affectionate manner. And he wasn't disgusted. No – Jesus' face was relaxed, with love shining through. It was like – it was like I was important. Not just some tag-a-long follower, to make the number of disciples a round twelve. But that I mattered to Jesus, that he cared about me so deeply and truly.

It was a little weird, in the way that Jesus' gestures sometimes are. Like, here we all were, waiting to begin eating, but Jesus took his time with each of us. When he first knelt down, to wash the feet of John Mark, I didn't really know what to do. I mean, you usually either wash your feet when you come into a building, or you don't bother at all. And it wasn't some random servant, but Jesus – the Teacher – the Master himself! So, we all mostly kept quiet. Well, everyone but Peter. He refused to let Jesus wash his feet.

Mary:

Well, that sounds like Peter.

Bartholomew:

Yeah, right? He told Jesus that he wasn't worthy to be washed. And Jesus said, and I quote, "Unless I wash you, you won't have a place with me."

Unless I wash you, you won't have a place with me. He might have said that to Peter, but I heard them, too. I mean, he hadn't washed my feet yet. Was I not welcome here? But, Jesus loves all of us – like you said, Jesus walks the path of love, and shows love and dignity to everyone he meets. So, then Peter says, "Wash not only my feet, but all of me." And Jesus kinda smiled, and looked at him like, "oh, Peter" – and said, "Those who have been bathed need only to have their feet washed, because they are completely clean." But then, his face fell, and he said, "You disciples are clean, but not every one of you."

When he said that – my heart sank. He had to be talking about me, right? He hadn't gotten to me yet, but I knew that this was it. I'm too quiet with the guys – I don't speak up much, except with Phillip. I even questioned if anything good could come out of Nazareth. Surely, he was talking about me. Even with all these thoughts swirling in my head, Jesus still eventually got to me. And that's when I saw his attention and his care, as he washed my feet. He knows me, he cares for me.

After he was through washing everyone's feet, he told us what the point was: "I have given you an example: Just as I have done, you must also do." You see – it's not just Jesus that's on this way of love – he wants us to follow him, to do what he does, to care for each other. That bit about "not every one of us is clean"? Later, he got more direct – he said that one of us would betray him, and Judas got up and left. But – Jesus washed Judas' feet, too! It got me thinking – he told us to love even our enemies. But it's more than that – we're to serve anyone who needs it, no matter what we think about them, no matter who they are.

Mary:

Some people are going to be a lot harder to love than others...

Bartholomew:

He wants us to overcome our pride, to trust in his way of love! He even said he had a new commandment for us – to love each other as he loves us – even when he's not with us. I guess that means we need to love each other with the same extravagance that you lavished on Jesus. To serve each other with the same humility and compassion that he showed us.

Mary:

>Bartholomew, do you hear that?

Bartholomew:

>What?

Mary:

>It sounds like…marching.

Bartholomew:

>Yes, it's…Roman soldiers! They have swords and torches…

Mary:

>Is that Judas with them? My God…

Bartholomew:

>Let's get out of here. Tell your family. Tell the other disciples! We can pray for Jesus once we're safe.

Mary:

>May God keep us all safe. [Both exit]

Soul Debt
(Rev. Lucus Keppel)
Amos 8: 4-7; Luke 16: 1-13

About fifty years ago, the first of the Baby Boomers that were college bound entered the walls of their educational institutions, and a great debate over the cost of college education began. After all, in 1960, you could barely support yourself in college with a minimum-wage part time job. The average price of tuition, fees, room and board in 2012 dollars, was $3500. Working part time, at minimum wage, you had to work twenty-five weeks to make that much money – leaving you little time at all for time outside of your studies. Debates raged for years, hands were wrung, and no legislation went into effect. Instead, colleges were free to set their own fees and tuition, despite receiving aid from the state both directly and in the form of tuition grants and loans.

By 1983, when Gen-X was off to college, the problem had gotten way out of hand. Costs nearly tripled – and how long do you think you now had to work, part time, minimum wage?

62 weeks to support one year of school. If you're not very math savvy, that means that you had to work MORE than a year to support that year's schooling. Ok, fine – but you made enough after graduation to pay off any debt you incurred, right? Absolutely. But the debate still raged, that tuition should be capped, and student loans should be offered. Of course, in 1987, legislation was passed that made it nearly impossible to discharge student loan debt in bankruptcy proceedings – the fear was that students would borrow more than they could afford, and then immediately declare bankruptcy.

That takes us to today – today, it takes nearly three years of working part time to pay for one year of college, and student debt has understandably ballooned as a result. In the USA, over 18 billion dollars is currently owed in student debt, and this amount just continues to increase, especially as more young people attend college, and businesses increasingly rely on a bachelor's degree as a gatekeeper to employment. And there is still no legislation limiting tuition increases, even as student debt is still incredibly difficult to discharge in bankruptcy.

To paraphrase Merle Travis and Tennessee Ernie Ford,[57]

---

[57] Tennessee Ernie. Ford, "Sixteen Tons," by Merle Travis, in *Sixteen Tons ; You Dont*

Y'study sixteen tomes, and what do you get? Another day older, and deeper in debt. Saint Peter, don'cha call me, 'cause I can't go: I owe my soul to my student loans.

While student debt is, admittedly, a modern phenomenon, the concept of unpayable debt is ancient. In the time after Solomon's rule of the kingdom of Israel, all debt, no matter when it was incurred, was to be forgiven every seven years, in the year of the jubilee. Additionally, every 49 years – seven times seven years – all of the land that had been sold to others was supposed to revert to its original owners. It's not really known how long this system functioned – or if it was only an ideal – but it is clear that the prophets raged against abuses of the system. For example, the prophet Amos talks about merchants who "trample the needy" and "destroy the poor of the land" with their deceptive practices.[58]

When you were driven by fortune or evil intent to need to take loans beyond your means to pay back, your final option was to sell yourself into slavery. To owe all of your labor to one person, who "bought the needy for silver." And you might well do this, expecting to be freed after seven years – or even fewer, with your debts forgiven and a clean slate before you. But those Amos is calling out would not forgive the debt – would not free their bond-slaves, even for as miniscule a price as a pair of sandals, or a bushel of grain. And so, Amos issues the chilling words of God: "Surely, I will never forget what they have done."

These bond-slaves were not uneducated – indeed, unlike the majority of the ancient peoples, most Israelite men could read and write in Hebrew, and many translated these skills over the years into Aramaic, Coptic Egyptian, and Koine Greek, or Latin. By Jesus' day, demand for these literate, numerically proficient slaves was very high. And, generally, they were valued by their masters, and given great freedom as overseers of great estates. Richard Vinson describes an overseer slave, the main character of a play by the ancient Roman Plautus, in this way:

> *His master has promised him a slave girl in marriage. [The overseer] has come to the city to gain his bride; when another slave accosts him for being away from his post, he replies, "I have not forgotten my duties; I left a manager [prefect] at the*

Have to Be a Baby to Cry. (Capitol Records, 1955) Vinyl recording.

[58] Amos 8:4-7

farm who will attend to its affairs properly, despite my absence."[59]

It seems, then, that as long as their work was well done, overseers had a great freedom of action.

It is an overseer of this type that Jesus describes in this Gospel story from Luke: "There was a certain rich man who had a manager handling his affairs," Jesus begins. Notice our only clue that the manager is a slave – that the rich man "has" a manager. As a side note, the word that we translate manager, steward, or overseer is *Oikonomos*,[60] a compound Greek word of *Oikos*, house, and *Nomos*, literally, lawyer, but with a subtle meaning of "one who makes laws" – that is, household manager. This is also the root of our English word "Economy" – the management of material resources. After all, the same skills that help run a household also can help run a kingdom, or nation – and we even refer today to micro-economy and macro-economy to emphasize their relatedness.

So, this manager of the household – in charge of the estate while the owner of the land is away - well, he has been accused of throwing away the master's stuff – literally, broadcasting it, scattering it like seed. Not surprisingly, the master tells him, "That's it; report to me on your management, 'cause you surely aren't managing my stuff anymore!" Except… this isn't a bright move. You don't tell the bookkeeper that you're firing them until you have the books in hand. And so, not wanting to get his hands dirty with manual labor, this manager comes up with a clever idea – he'll reduce the debt of everyone who owes the household, and thus secure a place with a debtor – or at least someone who will stand up for him! Thus, one person's debt is reduced in half, while another's is reduced by 20%. And in the end, Jesus says, "The rich man had to admire the dishonest rascal for being so shrewd."

If this ending has left you scratching your head, you're not alone. This passage is regularly called one of the most difficult parables to interpret – even Luke, the only Gospel writer to include it, gives three different interpretations, as though he's not sure which is right, either. But let's put on our context detective hats and investigate what is happening here – and what Jesus is saying to the disciples listening to this incredibly odd parable.

---

[59] Richard Vinson, "On Possessions (Luke 16)," in *Luke*, Vol. 21. Smyth & Helwys Bible Commentary (Macon: Smyth & Helwys Publishing, 2008), 521

[60] οἰκονόμος (oikonomos)

First of all, what is shrewd about this? Some commentators really work hard to explain that the manager was simply reducing the debt by his portion of it – his commission, if you will. But, this doesn't track with the amounts given – 400 gallons of oil? That's more than a commission on a debt.

Ok, but what about this: Jews weren't supposed to charge interest to other Jews, but interest could be hidden within the principal that was owed back. Maybe the manager is reducing this hidden interest? Maybe – this does account for the difference of 50% on one, 20% on the other – but, even if this practice were widespread – and we have no evidence that it was – there's not even a hint of it in the story.

Instead, here's my take: the manager is simply reducing people's debt. It's not quite the Jubilee of ancient Israel – they still owe something, after all – but he's just giving a huge break to the debtors. The daily wage of a field laborer would cover about 10 gallons of oil, so 400 gallons is about 40 days of work. Likewise, the value of the grain is about 150 days work – a smaller percentage, but a larger value. In this way, the manager is making it less likely that any of the debtors will have to sell themselves into slavery – or take other drastic measures – to pay back their debt and making it clear that he has their interest at heart. Additionally, he may be forcing the owner of the estate into a bind – after all, the owner has only the books to go on, which the manager is currently "fixing". If the owner wants to get the previous amount, he has to check with the debtors – who will likely only own up to the reduced value. Instead, if the owner "takes the credit", he looks generous – "so rich that he can cut his bills in half and still stay rich" as Richard Vinson puts it.[61]

So, in the end, this overseer has, despite his cheating, made things better for everyone. This is what Jesus is lifting up: Even dishonest people can do the right thing, by reducing debt, when it can benefit them. You disciples, then, ought to do the right thing, when it doesn't benefit you directly in this life. Give to everyone – not just your friends, but to all who need help. Reduce your debt, and the debts of others as much as you can.

Remember the student loan numbers I quoted before? $18 billion in debt seems like a huge amount – but it evens out to just $75 per adult in the US. Even if it were averaged across only those who went to college, that still is only $240 per person. We could, together, do a lot to mitigate the cost of college. To forgive debts that we collectively own – 90% of that 18 billion is owed not to private lenders, but to the government, or us collectively. Instead, we are crippling our young with debt that they will not be able to

---

[61] Vinson, *Luke* p. 522

repay and have no way for forgiveness. Rather than waiting for a crooked loan overseer to help us, we should take action in favor of a national jubilee, and actually work toward fair practices in tuition and education, to keep these debts from crippling each other. When we pray the Lord's Prayer, don't we ask for our debts to be forgiven as we forgive the debts of each other? What would happen if we started taking that seriously – not just forgiving each other's sins or trespasses, but their actual debts?

There are organizations doing this already – buying debt from collections agencies for pennies on the dollar and forgiving the full debt. But because student debt is protected from bankruptcy, it's also protected from being sold cheaply. No one of us can forgive debt alone – we're not in the position of the overseer from Jesus' parable – but together, we can work for justice and forgiveness, and celebrate jubilee.

May God's justice fill your heart with mercy. May Christ's example lead you to radical forgiveness. May the Holy Spirit fill us with the joy of reconciliation. Amen.

Prayers of the People

Is This Love?
(Rev. Elana Levy)
Song of Songs 8:6-7; Isaiah 53:3-6; Romans 5:1-5

I have a friend – I'll call her Lydia. She is one of those larger than life people – one of those people that you're just drawn to. She's been full of energy ever since she was a kid. Her mother had to sign her up for every class imaginable because otherwise she bounced off the walls. Which means, by the time I met her, she had several black belts, designed costumes, danced professionally, and other wild and wonderful things. But a lot changed for her. She started seeing this guy and he was becoming more and more abusive. Once, after a particularly terrible incident, we had a long talk in a diner. All revved up, but with no clue how she would make it, she left him. I told her that I would be there for her – for anything that she needed, any time day or night. But that weekend, she went back to him and I didn't see her for months.

She had moved into his house and followed him to clubs and parties, but she wasn't allowed anything else. One day out of the blue, their roommate called me worried. He said she had started blacking out and fainting and that the EMTs said there was nothing medically wrong with her. It happened so many times that they started to recognize her and wouldn't take her to the hospital any more. The roommate figured that I could tell him what to do to fix it. He was desperate, but he didn't challenge the abuse either.

Even though we hadn't spoken for months, I reached out to her again and she agreed to meet with me. She had to sneak out of the house in the morning while he was hungover, and we walked to a downtown park just a few blocks from their place. She didn't look like Lydia anymore. She was somehow…smaller. She couldn't look me in the eyes and there was something about her – she seemed to be trying to hide. We sat together in that park for several hours, sometimes not speaking. But I told her that I loved her; I told her that I missed her. She blankly told me stories about the abuse she was facing on a daily basis, but in between, she told me how he was not such a bad guy and how he was stressed because he lost his job. She worried about him and told me that she loved him even though she often didn't want to. I listened to her pain and her sorrow. I held her hand and in between stories I asked her, "Is this what love looks like?" I must have asked her that question a dozen times – not angrily, not as an accusation, but to try to help her to think of her life in a different way even if she wasn't ready to leave.

One of the most common questions that people ask about domestic violence is: why do victims stay with the abuser? This is a complex question, but a very important one if we want to understand how to work for justice with sensitivity and love. Relationships with abusers don't start out with abuse at full tilt. Like most on a first date, they present a very different face than what lies beneath. They can seem sensitive, kind, romantic, and devastatingly charming. They tend to start whirlwind romances where the couple finds themselves spending all their time together. And apart from occasional questionable words or deeds, they seem like any other relationship with good patches and bad patches. Some abusers even hold off until after marriage to show their true colors.

But there are some red flags even early on. Abusers might be controlling – telling their partners what to wear or who they're allowed to talk to or where they should go. They can be very jealous, and act easily hurt. But each of these things can be interpreted as romantic – jealousy proves he loves me; she likes how I look in this and wants me to be beautiful. Even insults can seem like a bridge to something good "you look ugly in that; why not wear what I got you?" These insults that can be explained away are only a bridge to far more intense emotional abuse.

The easiest way to understand how things go from relatively minor insults to abuse is to think of an abuser's tactics as being like brainwashing. They shift the blame for anything and everything to their partner – including their own angry moods and violence. In arguments, they deny any wrongdoing, they lie about what really happened, they twist things into an attack on their partner and others, they accuse others of their own faults. They generalize and exaggerate; they yell and shout over and interrupt their partners. They shame and humiliate their partners to break down their self-esteem and their sense of self. Then, they paint the world as a fearful place where their partner could never survive without them. However terrible the abuse seems, victims generally spend all of their energy just surviving day to day. The thought of a different life – a better life seems impossible. On top of all that, abusers typically isolate their partners from their friends and family. They want to shut out any voice or influence other than their own so that they can maintain control.

In the course of the relationship, abusers will lash out with abuse, but then follows a honeymoon period. They apologize, they swear they'll change, they act with some measure of kindness just long enough to convince their partner to stay. Then the tension rises once more. The victim learns to try to accommodate – try to do anything to prevent a moment of abuse or to get it over with quickly. And the longer the relationship lasts, the quicker this cycle turns. Victims have hope that that honeymoon person will stick around – that the change will be real this time. Victims often feel like their abuser really does need them and they dismiss their injuries as nothing, just as the abuser does. But they do truly feel trapped. In some cases, the victim may have the means or the support system to get out, but in others they are financially dependent on the abuser. Or they may fear for the well-being and safety of children if they try to leave.

Victims of domestic violence generally believe that it's their fault. Having been brainwashed, they believe that if they had been a perfect partner, they would not have suffered from a violent outburst. Often, they believe that the only way to survive is to be more loving, more nurturing, to make more excuses for the violence.

And here, within the sanctuary of our faith, we can ask, "is this love?" Is this the love that God calls us to when we read, "love your neighbor"? No. No. Absolutely not. But there are those who read our scriptures, who identify as Christians, who would pick out Bible verses to tell victims that God ordered their suffering. Some Christians would read the passage from Isaiah, which tells of the suffering servant and proclaim that if we are to follow Jesus then we will bear injuries just like he did. Or from Romans, "We also boast in our sufferings, knowing that suffering produces endurance, and endurance produces character, and character produces hope." Some would read that passage and say that it means that suffering is normal or even a good thing that strengthens our faith.

The Bible is our book. It belongs to all of us and it is filled with beautiful truths that propel us into the light and goodness in this world. Romans 5 goes on to tell us, "God's love has been poured into our hearts through the Holy Spirit that has been given to us." God's love is in our hearts and any who seek to block it out do not follow God.

I tell you now, God does not require suffering. Suffering is not something we seek out or inflict on others; if we are doing that, we are not serving God – we are serving a twisted master, indeed. Because when Paul talks about suffering – when Jesus talks about suffering, they are usually talking about persecutions in the early church. They are talking about what we suffer as a result of spreading the Gospel – of working in Jesus' name. We remember our history – in the early church, believers were beaten and stoned, tortured, imprisoned, and killed just for being Christian and spreading the faith of their own hearts to others. In John 16:33, Jesus says, "In the world you face persecution…" "in me you…have peace." God rescues from affliction – God rescued Joseph from slavery and Egypt from famine. Faith helps us to endure, faith helps us find strength and peace. Our hope is in God and God is greater than any abuser, any power, any evil in this world.

Domestic violence does not spread the gospel; it does not share God's love; it does not lift up or build up, or illuminate anything true. In the Bible, we don't just find ethical rules of what to do and what not to do. We don't just find stories of heroes and villains of faith. We also find passion and love to help guide our romantic selves. Many throughout history have looked at the Song of Songs and said, "why is this even part of scripture?" And there's a lot in this book that, well, might have made more sense in the romantic poetry of the day, but I think that this book is crucial. If we do not love well – if we do not know what love is then how can our houses be homes? And so, we find a beautiful poem of what romantic love really is. Our love poet tells us, "Set me as a seal upon your heart, as a seal upon your arm." Love is a sign of faithfulness, one heart connected intimately to another heart. But not just hidden deep in our chests – it's a seal on our arms, too. Love is proclaimed publicly, with joy in the presence of the beloved. Because, "love is strong as death, passion fierce as the grave." Love does not cause death; love does not wear away at the essence of the beloved. Real love, inspired by God, is unconquerable, it's enduring, it feeds both parties. This isn't to say that real love never changes – yes, we change, and we grow together; sometimes we grow apart. But real love is built on trust, a desire to see the best for the beloved, a celebration of all victories, and support through all difficulties.

When Lucus and I got married, we found another verse from Song of Songs that we liked a good deal. "I am my beloved's and my beloved is mine." *Ani l'dodi v'dodi li.*[62] It is here, on our wedding bands as a seal upon our fingers. We belong to one another – equally. We are responsible to God and to one another, and it is part of our calling to respect and honor that we are to be partners to one another.

When abusers redefine love for their victims, one of the most supportive things we can do for them is to ask them, "is this what love looks like?" Because it's okay if you can't leave just yet. It's okay if any other life seems impossible right now. All you need to know is that I love you; God loves you; and that will be constant and true no matter what you decide. As 1 John reminds us, "in this is love, not that we loved God, but that God loved us." And our song of scripture rings out, "Many waters cannot quench love, and

---

[62] אני לדודי ודודי לי (ani l'dodi v'dodi li)

rivers cannot sweep it away." Love abides, and real love is stronger than anything. Amen.

If You Had Been Here
(Rev. Elana Levy)
Revelation 21:1-6; John 11:32-44

I've worked as a bereavement counselor and I've suffered loss myself. Grief has got to be one of the hardest things we ever face in life, if not the hardest thing. It's not just that we feel sad – grief can have every possible feeling wrapped up in it and it can shift at the blink of an eye. We can be relieved, guilty, nostalgic, angry, anxious, or giddy. Grief can slow us down – physically and mentally – making us feel isolated from everyone and from the life we were used to living. Unlike most problems that we face in life, grief doesn't come with an easy fix. If we get into debt, want to go back to school, get into a fight with someone dear – we can always try to take steps to achieve our goals and repair relationships. But when we're grieving, there's nothing we can do to bring that person back. We cannot make things like they used to be.

This, alone, would be enough – too much, even. But grieving is more difficult because it's hard to find people who will listen, stick by you, see you through the tough times. Death is hidden in our culture. We're not supposed to talk about it, we don't see it around us, and, when grief comes along, we often have no idea how to cope with it.

On top of that, we might have some theological guilt infused into our mourning. I once had this client. I can't remember whose death she was grieving, but it was someone she was very close to – her mother or her spouse. She had waited more than six months to come in and talk to someone. Finally, she came in because she just felt stuck. Here grief surrounded her and she still wasn't able to reengage in her life. After a couple of a sessions, she told me about an encounter she had had with her pastor. He called her into his office and she had no idea why. After a few pleasantries, he indicated that he wanted to talk about her grieving. He rebuked her for being sad. He told her that, as a Christian, it was totally inappropriate to be sad or in pain because it meant that she lacked faith. According to him, if she were a good Christian she would have real hope in Jesus and that would overwhelm any possible bit of sadness she might feel.

I couldn't believe my ears. I was so angry for her and wanted to march straight to that pastor's study and give him a piece of my mind. But she, she took his words to heart. She decided that she must be faithless, that she must be truly alone. She stopped going to church and she just stayed home. I wanted to point her to Christian hope and the boundless compassion of Jesus

Christ that would never try to shame her for how she felt. But I was there as a therapist and not as a pastor.

So many times, in funerals or when we try to comfort one another, we speak as though it's not okay to mourn – that it's some kind of failing. But in the Gospel of John, Jesus has been called to Bethany by some good friends of his, Mary and Martha, because their brother Lazarus has died. Mary falls to the ground at Jesus' feet – she can't believe that he didn't come earlier, she can't believe that he didn't save her brother's life. Jesus sees everyone's mourning – family and friends – and he is, "deeply moved in spirit and troubled." He groans to himself and he gets upset to see so many people hurting. He asks to see the body of his good friend and, for once, the people tell Jesus, "come and see." When he sees Lazarus, Jesus starts to weep.

Scripture doesn't tell us what Jesus was feeling or why. It doesn't say whether Jesus knew that he would have the strength and the power to raise Lazarus up. But in that moment, Jesus came face to face with the loss of his friend and he wept. Even if he knew that Lazarus would be raised by Jesus' own hand, in that moment, Jesus was pained to see his friend taken from his earthly life. Jesus did not scold those around him for mourning their friend and brother. He joined them in their sorrow; he was a companion in their journey through the valley of the shadow of death.

And even in the midst of grief, we can sense that this isn't all that there is. We know Jesus better than to think that he's every entirely done with any of us. The story is not over yet. Mary's words at the beginning of the Gospel lesson may well echo how we feel during the sorrow of loss, "Lord, if you had been here, my brother would not have died." Lord, why did you take her so soon? Lord, why did she have to suffer? You can do all things, surely you could have kept him from dying.

I do not believe that these are the questions of someone who has no faith or someone whose faith is weak. We believe in Jesus Christ – we look for him working in our world and in our lives. When someone we love is hurt, we reach out to our Lord and savior for the healing and the miracle that only he can provide. And if it doesn't come, we can be left with this emptiness – Lord, if only you had been there.

But here, in the Gospel, we find that Jesus is just as moved, just as mournful as we are. Jesus is not apathetic, distracted by other things, or uninterested in our most earnest prayers. He sees the very real pain that comes from someone departing this life. And by his weeping, he tells us most assuredly: I was there; I am here; I have always been there.

Just as Jesus is there for us in our grief, he is there for those we love who have gone home to be with him. Before Jesus raises Lazarus from the dead, he says, "Did I not tell you that if you believe, you will see the glory of God?" Jesus wants us to trust him – even through death. Because Jesus never lets any of us go. In raising Lazarus, Jesus gave the first sign that he is Lord of life and of death; that if he can heal the blind and raise the dead, he can raise each faithful soul to glory with him.

And Jesus, who himself weeps with us, tells us that we are going to a holy city, created anew by God to dwell together in peace. The book of Revelation tells us, "God will be with the people; God will wipe every tear from their eyes. Death will be no more; mourning and crying and pain will be no more, for the first things have passed away.'" While we are in this life, mourning and crying and pain are burdens that we must bear, signs of loving and caring for others when they depart from us. But when we are in heaven, there will be nothing more to mourn. All things will be new, completely fulfilled. Jesus is truly the beginning and the end, the one Source that can quench every thirst and need.

It's hard to be in this in between place. It's hard to know the perfect paradise that awaits us and to live in a world with such brokenness and sorrow. It's hard to let go of the people we love the most – even into the hands of our Lord and Savior; even knowing that they are at peace. But I tell you now, that we are part of the church and Jesus Christ is our head. And it's not just us down here who make up the church. Those who have gone on to be with Jesus are the church triumphant. All of the saints living and dead, in heaven and in earth are part of the church universal, the mystical body of Christ. And that means that it is crowded in the church and on earth.

Have you ever noticed that? Look to you left and your right – above you and all around. This place is filled with the saints of the church, praying us forward, singing songs of praise right along with us. Saints are dancing down the aisles and rejoicing in holy worship. Those we love who have died are not lost – they're right here in our worship, in our lives, and in our hearts.

So, friends, when you face grief, remember that you are not alone. If you would weep, weep with Christ. If you are weighed down by sorrow, drained of energy, let Scripture be your companion. If you are filled with stories of memories happy and sad, share them in the company of saints that we may get to know more of the souls that we will meet in the great by and by.

Mourning is not our shame, it is the way that we love when we face death. And here, surrounded by all the saints, let us take strength from their faith and from the example of their lives. Let us bring out the best of their wisdom and legacy in our actions. Let us feel freedom in Christ to come as we are and to lift each other up come what may. Amen.

The Sacraments:
Baptism and Holy Communion

Being the Beloved Child
(Rev. Lucus Keppel)
Isaiah 42: 1-9; Matthew 3:13-17

We are living in an amazing time, my friends. Technological marvels surround us – why, just this week, I was able to have a conversation spanning from Alaska to Tulsa to Detroit and even to London, Shanghai, and Jakarta. Last month, our webmaster Erik reported that the church's website – trinitychurchbixby.org – was visited by people in 20 different states! There was a time when visitors from 20 different states would have had to coordinate to visit a church – now, it's easy, and happens almost seamlessly.

Let me show you something else that's amazing – this is an image of the work of the artist Sam Van Aken.[63] He has taken an ancient art and science – horticulture – and found a way to graft stone-fruit trees together. Not just two or three – this is his *Tree of Forty Fruit*. Forty different fruit, all grafted onto the same trunk, sharing the same sap, and the same nutrients. In the spring, it bursts out into a riot of color and in the summer, like this picture, its fruit is free for the picking. All forty different kinds – planted together for the enjoyment of everyone, whether you have gold – or locusts. Sam Van

---

[63] Sam Van Aken, *Tree of 40 Fruit*. July 17, 2013. Ronald Feldman Fine Art. https://commons.wikimedia.org/wiki/File:Tree_of_40_Fruit_-_nursery_-_DSC_0302.jpg.

Aken has planted over a hundred of these trees so far, in the green areas of cities as far reaching as New York City to Portland, Oregon, and he's done his best to ensure that the trees will be cared for. As it happens, they don't need any more care than a fruit tree of a single variety – once the grafted branches are secure, it's like they are one tree, despite their radically different origins.

The Tree of Forty Fruits is the sort of righteous project that I love to see. Something that offers food for the hungry – for everyone who is hungry. Righteousness, you see, is a combination of justice and mercy. Yes, we may not quite use it that way in English, but the theological concept pre-dates English, so we're going with the older meaning here! Justice and mercy combined to make righteousness. That's the kind of righteousness Jesus describes when he says – "Allow me to be baptized now. This is necessary to fulfil all righteousness."[64] To fulfil the combination of justice and mercy, Jesus had John baptize him. When Jesus tells the disciples in the Great Commission to "go therefore to all nations, making disciples, baptizing them in the name of the Father, the Son, and the Holy Spirit,"[65] he's telling them – and us – to baptize in righteousness, too. To be "baptized in the name of God" means to be chosen to follow in God's way. To be a little Christ – a Christian – and to be filled with the Holy Spirit as Jesus was.

"But, Pastor Lucus!" (you might say) "I was baptized as a baby, so I don't remember it all that well – but I'm pretty sure that every baptism I've seen since didn't end up with the heavens opening, a dove descending, and God calling out "This is my Son, whom I dearly love. I find happiness in him!""

To which I can only respond – "Are you sure? Because you're certainly familiar with those words!"

As you may know, three of the gospels tell the story of Jesus' baptism, and the fourth at least mentions that Jesus was baptized by John, even if it doesn't tell the story directly. In Mark, the earliest of the gospels to be written, God's voice and descending dove of the Spirit appear only to Jesus.[66] Luke follows suit,[67] leaving only the gospel of Matthew to have God publicly claim Jesus at his baptism. Yet, it's at this moment in Jesus' life, as he rose from the

---

[64] Matthew 3:13-17 (CEB)

[65] Matthew 28:16-20 (NRSV)

[66] Mark 1:9-11

[67] Luke 3:21-22

waters at John's urging, that the people first hear about Jesus as God's beloved Son, and the Spirit manifests with him.

The form of a dove, by the way, is not a usual symbol for the Spirit in the Hebrew Bible. Instead, the dove usually represented the people of Israel themselves – they found identity with the dove sent out by Noah, who returned in peace, carrying an olive branch – representing fruitfulness. Later, in the exile, they found comfort in the mournful cry of the dove, as the Prophets Isaiah and Ezekiel relate.[68] Doves were also sacrificed for atonement in the Temple – and the Talmud and various Targums compares the binding of Isaac to the way doves stretch out their necks before a sacrifice. So, doves represented atonement, sacrifice, mourning, return, and the people of Israel – and later, the Holy Spirit.

The mourning cry of the dove in exile brings us to verses from Isaiah. God says to the people:

> *You, Israel, my servant, I have chosen you and will not cast you off, fear not, for I am with you, be not dismayed, for I am your God.*[69]

When we get to the next chapter, then, it is read in the context of the exile, with the Servant being (at least originally) identified as the people of Israel. When God says, "My Servant won't cry out, or shout aloud, or make his voice heard in public," the term "cry out" is the same used for the mournful cry of the dove. We also see God saying, "Here is my servant, my chosen, my beloved, who brings me delight. I've put my Spirit on him, he will bring justice to the nations." Remember, this originally meant the people of Israel – no longer would they cry out like a dove, because they would bring justice to the nations, and delight to God.

When Jesus is baptized in the gospel of Matthew, God makes these same claims – that had been general – specific to Jesus. "This is my Son, my beloved, in whom I have delight." The Spirit descends to Jesus in the form of the dove - which meant the whole people of Israel – and if you turn the metaphorical page, immediately leads Jesus into the wilderness for the Temptation, just as the Hebrew people had been led into the wilderness after God reminded them of God's love for them through Moses in Egypt. What

---

[68] Isaiah 28, Ezekiel 7

[69] Isaiah 41: 8-10 (RSV, Truncated)

had been general became specific in Matthew's Gospel – and then general again at the Great Commission.

You see, when you are baptized in the name of God the Father, Christ the Son, and the Holy Spirit, you descend with Jesus into the depths of watery chaos, and rise again with Jesus, into the same Spirit and the same promise of God that Jesus did. John Calvin compared this to being grafted into Christ – your own branch on the shoot of Jesse, the mighty trunk that nourishes you with the same nourishment of your neighbor branches.[70] Yes, you might be an apricot, and your neighbor a plum – but you're both nourished and supported by the great trunk of Christ. If you were baptized as a child, it's because your family knew even then that God had called you a beloved child and wanted to recognize that publicly. If you were baptized as a youth or adult, you made that same statement – that God has called you, and that God has loved you from the very beginning. If you have never been baptized, don't worry – God calls you a beloved child, also. The Sacrament of Baptism is a public recognition of that love, and an acknowledgement of that grafting, not the act that grafts.

When we are called to remember our baptism, we are called to remember not only that we are connected, like the branches of the Tree of 40 fruit, but what we are called to do because of that connection. In the Servant Song of Isaiah, God goes on to tell us what that is:

> *I, the Lord, have called you for a good reason. I will grasp your hand and guard you, and give you as a covenant to the people, as a light to the nations, to open blind eyes, to lead the prisoners from prison, and those who sit in darkness from the dungeon.*[71]

The first step to overcoming darkness is to open your eyes – and help those around you open their eyes. See the beauty of the tree of life, whose trunk is Jesus, whose branches are you, your neighbor, and everyone's neighbor stretching back and forward in time – whose nourishment is the Spirit, and whose light is God. Fulfil all righteousness, you beloved child of God – act in justice and mercy, and you will do right by God, and remember, truly, your baptism – the same baptism of Jesus Christ.

---

[70] John Calvin, "Romans 6: 5-6," *Commentaries on the Epistle of Paul the Apostle to the Romans*, trans. John Owen (Grand Rapids: Christian Classics Ethereal Library, 1539) https://www.ccel.org/ccel/calvin/calcom38.x.iii.html

[71] Isaiah 42: 6-7 (CEB)

May you be bathed in God's light, that you grow good fruit. May you hold tight to your baptism in Jesus, that you follow his Way. May you be so nourished by the Holy Spirit, that you know, truly, that you are a beloved child of God. Amen.

Hlāfweard
(Rev. Elana Levy)
Exodus 16:4a, 9-15; Mark 4:26-29; John 6:31-35

When I was little, we would celebrate Shabbat in our home because my father is Jewish. Dad would go to a bakery and get an enormous loaf of challah – a braided egg bread. After a few years, someone got my mother a bread machine. My brother and I decided that we would find a recipe and bake our own special bread. We let the machine prepare the dough, but we took it out before the baking cycle so that we could roll the dough into three long snakes, braid it ourselves, and pop it into the oven. The tantalizing scent of that bread breaking curled through the house and whet our appetites for our Friday supper. When I went away to college, I lost my weekly bread making tradition and I stopped going to church. After five or six years, the church started calling me to come back, to seek God more earnestly. I went on a mission trip to New Orleans and I heard that a woman from our host church baked the communion bread every time. Somehow, it had never occurred to me that someone could actually bake bread, non-professionally for a church. So, I asked my pastor if he would let me bake the communion bread – if the challah of my childhood would be okay to make. He said that sounded great, so I found a new job in the church.

I found the old recipe, I found videos online, I listened to the ever sage, ever hilarious advice of Alton Brown. Doing the same recipe over and over again led to certain adjustments and refinements – using boiling water for steam heat during the rising stage, preparing and baking the dough at church so it was fresh from the oven, learning a six-strand rather than a three-strand braid. Every Sunday we had communion, the sweet smell of bread filled the halls of the building and you could hear people come in the church doors, take a big 'ol whiff of the air, and say, "are we having communion today?" Suddenly in our little North Carolina church, communion became something different for all of us. We anticipated it, we missed it on Sundays when we didn't have it. People (myself included) came up to the Table salivating for that warm, filling, holy food. After the service, many of the congregants would swarm the kitchen to grab extra helpings.

Lucus and I made the communion bread recently at our church in Bixby, Oklahoma. (If I'm being totally honest, it was mostly Lucus.) From behind the table, he and I could both see some of that same anticipation from our church family: surprise that it was still warm, eagerness to take the bread – indeed, together we can all, "taste and see that the Lord is good." At the holy table, we can enter into a sort of compressed time: we are at table with Christ, with all the saints, past and present, with our childhood selves, with ourselves in the future. This grace-filled place is where we find infinite connection: up to God and across to all the world.

Many scriptures center around bread: manna as the bread of heaven, Jesus as the bread of life, the growing grain that bursts forth all over to signify the kingdom of God. It is certainly no accident that bread and wine are so intertwined with the center of our faith. In Jesus' day, they were the staple food and drink – they were common food shared by the poor and the wealthy. Even the simplest, most taken for granted things can be transformed in God's holiness into what the reformers used to call "means of grace." A simple speech, with God's help, becomes a sermon, a way we can more deeply experience God's grace. So can a loaf, a cup, a stream of water. They are specially ordained by God to show us who we are and whose we are.

In the wilderness wanderings, the people fainted for want of bread, so God rained down manna from the sky. They didn't know what it was, but Moses confirmed to them that this was the bread from God. God chose the people, chose to sustain the people, and provided holy bread – flaky and lightly sweet like honey. Following God, they were provided for – even when their faith and trust wavered.

In our parable from Mark, Jesus is on a roll (no pun intended). He's in the middle of several different stories about the kingdom of God – what is it like, how will we know it, who's getting in, what do we do? He starts with the much more familiar seed parable about sowing seeds on the path, on the rocky ground, and in the good soil. He explains to his followers that they've received the, "secret of the kingdom of God" so they need to understand the deeper meaning of what he is saying. Be receptive to the word of God and bear fruit; don't put your lamp under a bushel; the kingdom of God is like a mustard seed (though small, it makes a mighty tree). And here is our little parable of the growing seed right in the middle. It's not in any of the other Gospels. We could almost call it the parable of the bad farmer. I mean, what kind of serious gardener would plant seeds and then totally ignore them? Go to sleep and wake up and not contribute to the care or tending of the plants whatsoever?! We can be fairly certain that the sower here is not supposed to be God or Jesus or Spirit – God isn't an inactive, passive observer of our faith.

I think that this parable is looking at how the kingdom of God arrives. We know that no matter how much work that we do, real spiritual growth and nourishment come from God. We can't make it grow, make it become what we want, how we want, when we want. God gives the seeds and God makes the growth. So much of what happens is hidden from us – a mystery. But just as we can trust that a planted seed quite often becomes a plant and bears fruit, we can also hold on to our faith that God is working all the time, that the Spirit is molding the stalk and the head of the grain. We can show up and tend the land and try to make things happen on our own time, but the coming of the grain, the coming of the kingdom is in God's hands. This grain, this staple of life, will not fail us.

And so, we come to Jesus the bread of life. He reminds us that true bread comes from heaven. What we need to survive, what we need for faithfulness and righteousness and life – all of that comes from God. Jesus reminds us that if we come to him, we will never go hungry and if we believe in him, we will never be thirsty. Knowing that Jesus is the true bread inspires us to hunger for nothing else, to thirst for no one else.

Our earliest Christian statement of faith was a simple one: "Jesus is Lord." In many ways, I think it's deceptively simple. We could say it means Jesus is Lord, as in Jesus is God. Easy-peezy. Or we could think of Lord as in, "Lord and Master." Jesus is our master who is in charge of our lives and who we owe our loyalty. Pretty good theology there. But, of course, we also think of Lords and Ladies – fancy British rich people who may be too good for commoners like us. That's… not as good for describing Jesus. Or there's the feudal Lord who has countless serfs who are worked to the bone and not paid fairly, subject to the cruel whims of the boss. I certainly hope we don't see Jesus that way.

It turns out that the word *Lord* comes from an Old English compound word that I will almost certainly mispronounce: *hlāfweard*. *Hlāf* is where we get the word "loaf" from: *hlāf*, loaf. Those sound pretty close. *Weard* is not "weird" like a person who is strange and not normal. It's closer to "ward" as in someone who guards or keeps or protects. So, *Lord* is "the keeper of the bread," "the one who protects the bread." The word came from an old Germanic tribal custom that it was the chieftain who provided the food for those who followed him.[72] Originally, the word wasn't that prevalent. The *Lord* word they used to use for a god was *drighten*, which meant a ruler with an army – someone who commanded a violent force.[73] But somewhere between the 5th and the 7th century, the church chose a different word to use

---

[72] "Lord," in *Wikipedia: The Free Encyclopedia*, Wikimedia Foundation Inc., updated 3 September 2018, https://en.wikipedia.org/wiki/Lord.

[73] "Drighten," in *Wikipedia: The Free Encyclopedia*, Wikimedia Foundation Inc., updated 22 August 2018, https://en.wiktionary.org/wiki/drighten#English

for Lord in English.[74] Rather than lift up a warring leader (*drighten*), they chose the Lord who keeps the bread safe and gives it to his followers. They chose the word that depicted one in authority, but also the one who provides.

You can trace the journey of *Lord* back through its roots and find that in the old church Latin, *Dominus* could mean "one who subdues," but it could also mean, "one who builds a house." It was the one in charge, but also the host of a feast.[75] Then there's *kyrie*[76] from Greek. When the people say to Jesus, "sir, give us this bread always!" they say *kyrie*. It was their way of saying, "sir" or "mister," but it was also the way that Lord had been translated from the Old Testament in the Septuagint (which was a translation of the Bible from the 3rd century BC). So *kyrie* was a respectful way to address someone, a master or ruler, and the head of a household – responsible for caring for the needs of all.[77] From *kyrie* we go back to *Adonai*[78], the Hebrew word for Lord (as in Lord God) and mister. The earliest root of that comes from an ancient language called Ugaritic and it was probably Ad – father.[79]

Jesus is Lord – Jesus is the bread and he's the one who keeps the bread. He is one with the Father who provides for us and cares for us – giving even his own body to nourish us and save us. He is the bread and he protects it – he gives us life and holds our souls and heals our hearts so that we might be restored to God. Jesus is the bread from heaven with endless authority and power who, nevertheless, hosts the feast, heals our wounds, and breaks forth into the world in times and places where we least expect it.

As we think of fathers, some of us are fortunate to have relationships with fathers who stood by us, supported us, worked to equip us for life, and sent us out into the world. Others of us can scarcely imagine a positive experience of fatherhood because theirs was so painful. In our passages this morning, we find God providing for us no matter what our experience, no matter what

---

[74] "Lord," in *Wiktionary: The Free Dictionary*, Wikimedia Foundation Inc., updated 25 July 2018, https://en.wiktionary.org/wiki/lord.

[75] "Dominus," in *Wiktionary: The Free Dictionary* Wikimedia Foundation Inc., updated 25 July 2018 https://en.wiktionary.org/wiki/lord

[76] Κύριε (kyrie)

[77] "Kyrie," in *Wiktionary: The Free Dictionary*, Wikimedia Foundation Inc., updated 18 July 2018 https://en.wiktionary.org/wiki/kyrie.

[78] אֲדֹנָי (Adonai)

[79] "Adon," in *Wikipedia: The Free Encyclopedia*, Wikimedia Foundation Inc., updated 30 June 2018, https://en.wikipedia.org/wiki/Adon.

we might think we deserve. Though all might fall away, God never will. Though all might seem hopeless, we trust that Jesus is Lord. We stand together in that hope until the coming of the kingdom of God.

And we know that it is here, and we know that it is coming. At the end of Mark's parable, he says that, "when the grain is ripe…the harvest has come." This tense in Greek isn't one we really have in English. It describes an action that was completed in the past but has ongoing results that continue to affect the present and the future. The harvest began, the harvest is coming now, and the harvest continues to come, bringing the kingdom of God into being. The bread that gives life to the world, the bread of heaven in the triune God set the course toward heaven, towards fullness, and towards life eternal for all the saints. It was done, and it is unfolding for us every day. The kingdom of heaven is the surprise harvest, it is the bread offered by Jesus, it is the life shared together around the table, it is the joyful lordship that protects us and feeds us and sustains us this day and always. My friends, hear and believe the good news: Jesus is Lord. Amen.

I AM the Network
(Rev. Lucus Keppel)
John 15: 1-8; I John 4:7-21

Throughout the Gospel of John, Jesus uses a phrase beginning with I AM seven times:

> ** I AM the Bread of Life*
> ** I AM the Light of the World*
> ** I AM the Door*
> ** I AM the Good Shepherd*
> ** I AM the Resurrection and the Life*
> ** I AM the Way, the Truth, and the Life*
> ** I AM the True Vine*

As a quick refresher, one of the understandings of the Divine Name used throughout the Hebrew Bible is I AM. When Moses asks God in the burning bush who he should say sent him, God replies, "I AM that I AM."[80] So, John is making a point to have Jesus claim this name for himself – that Jesus is claiming unity with Divinity. And it gets better, too – five of the seven I AM statements that Jesus makes are of simple, everyday things that the people of his time knew and understood both practically. Jesus' statements make these simple, practical concepts have a deeper theological meaning – and referenced and subtly changed their existing theological meaning, if they had any.

The five everyday things are Bread, Light, Door, Shepherd, and this chapter's focus: The True Vine. Jesus uses these everyday practical ideas to help unpack difficult concepts, shedding light on the mystery of the Divine while keeping everything in good focus for ordinary people, like us.

Let's take a closer look at this grapevine image that Jesus uses in our scripture passage from today. In the ancient world, the grapevine was used along with palm branches as a national symbol for an Israel that was independent of foreign control – an Israel completely reliant on God. The Prophets Isaiah, Jeremiah, and Ezekiel use the image of the vine that produces wild grapes as a metaphor for God's people going astray: instead of producing the sweet grapes that were planted and planned for, it's clear that something has gone

---

[80] Exodus 3:14

horribly wrong. For the prophets, the sweet grapes that God has planted represent justice, while the wild grapes represent bloodshed. Isaiah uses the vineyard both directions – at first, the true vineyard, worth an incalculable fortune is overgrown with briars and thorns[81] – but later, after the exile to Babylon, Isaiah comforts the people with a promise that God will protect and care for the vineyard, preventing thorns and briars from growing.[82]

Much later in history, when the Maccabean revolt in Israel had succeeded and overthrown their Greek overlords, silver and copper coins were minted with images of palm branches and grapevines representing the newly independent state. Yet, by Jesus' day over a century later, the dream of independence had burst again. Now, the provinces of Syria and Palestine were under Roman control – first, under a loose arrangement with a local *Ethnarch*, or Peoples' King, and later integrated into the Roman system of provinces under a governor. If ever there was a time that a vineyard overgrown could represent Israel, it was then! After all, even the high priest was strictly regulated by the Roman authorities.

So, when Jesus refers to himself as the "True Vine," he's saying that he is the vine that bears the good fruit of justice, and not the overgrown vine that turns out bloodshed from sour grapes and thorns. That following in Jesus' way is a rebellious act against the status quo – against the powers that control, harm, and oppress. Jesus' way, remember, is not violent, but a sacrificial love. Not about gaining human power, but about recognizing that God wants human power to be used for the benefit of others. The corruption of goodness inherent in humanity needs to be pruned away so that, once again, God's sweet grapes of justice can grow and flourish in all the world.

And all that from referencing the True Vine – not to mention that Jesus later uses the result of pressed grapes – wine – as a way to speak about his blood at Communion.

Now, the grapevine is a symbol that has weight in many places for similar reasons. Vineyards have existed for a long time, and many people in many places have taken pride in their cultivation of grapes and wine. Perhaps one of the stranger examples of the grapevine as a symbol, though, has little to do with vineyards at all! In the mid-19th Century, just prior to the American Civil War, telegraph wires had been strung all across the United States, and especially along the railroads. To many, the telegraph poles and their slack

---

[81] Isaiah 7:23

[82] Isaiah 27:3

wires looked especially like a grape trellis and were fondly referred to as "grapevines." These grapevines represented progress – swift communication across long distances, news and even personal letters being able to be received just about as quickly as they were sent.

But during the civil war, the slang "Grapevine telegraph" switched its meaning – instead of referring to the telegraph wires, the grapevine telegraph now meant people talking to each other directly – the so-called, "real grapevine." So when someone said, "I heard it on the grapevine," the meaning came to be more about people talking to each other than through the telegraph. Amusingly, even then, the expression had it that you could hear more about the progress of the war from the grapevine telegraph than from the offices of Western Union!

Here's a good challenge for us all! Take a bit of time to listen for the Holy Spirit at work in you, and think about what common, everyday experiences in your life could point to God. Maybe you're not as familiar with kneading dough and baking bread, for example – or haven't shepherded a flock of sheep in your life. But you might be a teacher, and know that Jesus would say to you, I AM the Good Administrator – or Noble Professor – or the True Smartboard. Or maybe you're an Engineer, and Jesus would say to you, I AM the Good Mechanic – or the Friction of the World – or the True CPU. Really think on it - it's a good conversation starter!

To give you an example of how fun this can be, here's mine. Now, I'm not claiming this to be perfect, since I have no way of knowing for sure what Jesus would say today. However, this feels right:

> *I AM the Network – You are the Smartphones.*

After all, God connects us to each other – the loved ones and the wrong numbers.

We build cell towers not because God needs them, but as a visible symbol of God's signal in the world. For God's connection to us all does not require wires – and God's presence is felt even when we're not seeking it. God tends the network, reaching out and calling you at the most unexpected moments.

Now, the connection is always 4 bars strong – but we sometimes ignore the connection strength, ending the call while claiming we're going out of range, or through a tunnel. But no matter how long we turn on airplane mode, the signal is still there, waiting for us to return.

God facilitates conversation, whether late night long-distance chats, or simple texts of affirmation and love. I think God's wireless grapevine is always filled with Good News.

In God's network, we are accepted and loved from the moment we are assembled, and God holds our records safe, so that we can return in upgraded phones one day.

In Baptism, we recognize that no matter where we start out, we are always immersed in the love and grace of God.

At the communion table, we renew our contract with God. It's a plan that is offered free of charge in perpetuity. In the bread, we remember that we are part of one network – and in the cup, we remember that God's network calls us to reconcile and love each other.

May the God of all the World call you in the midst of the network. May Christ's love drive out fear in you. And may the Holy Spirit inspire you to stay connected to God and to each other. Amen.

Out-of-this-World Communion
(Rev. Lucus Keppel)
Psalm 8; 1 Corinthians 15: 35-44

On July 20, 1969, the whole story of humanity changed forever. On that day, Neil Armstrong and Eugene "Buzz" Aldrin successfully landed on the moon, becoming the first humans ever to step foot on *ground* that was not synonymous with *earth*. It was the culmination of years of engineering and psychology; the great triumphs and bitter loss that marked – and marks – humanity's space programs.

No one was entirely certain what Armstrong and Aldrin would face – they were both given instructions to fill a pouch on their leg with soil immediately after landing, just in case they had to leave the surface quickly. The whole way down, they struggled with alarm after alarm, and missed their target landing site by miles. Just before touching down, the computer gave them an erroneous low-fuel signal, due to the liquid fuel sloshing in the tank and uncovering a sensor. This was all on top of an already high-stress operation – and due to missing their target site, Armstrong landed the craft manually, with Aldrin calling out the navigation data. Above them, the Apollo 11 command/service module orbited the moon with its pilot, Michael Collins still inside, watching and relaying their transmissions just in case their lunar module's radio failed to reach Earth. Everyone was hoping for success in their mission, but they were prepared for failure. President Nixon even had a speech written that he was ready to deliver in the event of mission failure – but fortunately, he never had to give it. Instead, the first steps on a heavenly body were broadcast internationally, and Neil Armstrong's words would echo around the globe – "That's one small step for [a] man; one giant leap for mankind"

Long before the first moon landing, humanity gazed up at the night sky and marveled at the beauty of the heavenly lights. The multitude of stars, whirling overhead in dizzying, yet predictable patterns became an example of God's majesty and glory. As the psalmist puts it,

> *When I look at the night sky and see the work of your fingers – the moon and the stars you set in place – what are mere mortals that you should think about them, human beings that you should care for them?* [83]

---

[83] Psalm 8:3-4 (NLT)

I love how the psalmist uses a familiar phrase – the work of your hands – and tweaks it to the "work of your fingers." God's fingers, the psalmist seems to be saying, are used for the delicate work of placing stars in the sky, like the fingers of weavers, skilled and rapid, delicate and precise. Why the stars are placed where they are, the psalmist leaves as a mystery. Humanity is small in stature and number beneath the night sky, yet has been "crowned with glory and honor," "putting all things under their authority" – "flocks, herds, wild animals, birds of sky, fish of the sea, and everything in the ocean." Above us lies God alone – and yet, in the words of Stan Lee, "with great power there must also come great responsibility."[84]

In the psalmist's day, authority over the living things was evident. Humanity had tamed wild beasts, ideally taking care of their needs in exchange for their labor – but we were still captive to natural forces. The seas held the terror of chaos and the unknown, leading to the popular understanding that God's order only existed because God had conquered the chaos monster that had been in the sea, called Tiamat by the Babylonians. Indeed, Psalm 8 contains a veiled reference to this chaos monster of the depths – "You have taught children and infants to tell of your strength, silencing your enemies, and all who oppose you." "All who oppose you" is a fairly wide translation – the Hebrew is more literally, "to put an end to enemy and avenger."

By the modern era, the vast expanse of the sea and the air above both swarmed with human craft, travelling to-and-fro. Though we still know comparatively little about the depths of the sea, it no longer fills us with the same fear as it did our ancestors. Likewise, outer space beckons to us to explore beyond the skies above – and, just as we held authority and responsibility over the plants and animals of Earth, so we now hold authority over the building blocks of creation. Thermodynamics, nuclear and quantum physics, biotechnology and nanotechnology – we understand more about how creation holds together, and how to adjust it to our needs. Yet, even as our knowledge has grown, our need for wisdom to accompany it has grown apace. For although the psalmist holds humanity as crowned with glory and honor, the psalmist also notes that we are indeed lower than God. That no matter how far we explore, God's majestic name is there before us, filling earth and the heavens beyond.

---

[84] Stan Lee, "Spider-Man!" Comic strip. *Amazing Fantasy #15* (August 1962.) This was the popularization of the quote, originally attributed in sense (but not form) to an unknown French author in 1793 within the decrees of the French National Convention. https://quoteinvestigator.com/2015/07/23/great-power/

That's where the story of the first moon landing is so amazing. You see, before Neil Armstrong's historic first step, a less-well-known event took place within the lunar module on Tranquility base. Buzz Aldrin, an ordained ruling elder of Webster Presbyterian Church in Webster, Texas, unzipped his small pouch of personal items that each lunar astronaut was allowed to carry, and removed a sealed communion chalice and bread carried from the communion table blessed in worship, as well as an index card with John 15:5 written on it. He set the items before him, while Neil Armstrong looked on, and sent the following transmission to earth:

> *This is the LM pilot.*[85] *I'd like to take this opportunity to ask every person listening in, whoever and wherever they may be, to pause for a moment and contemplate the events of the past few hours and to give thanks in his or her own way.*[86]

In the silence that followed, Buzz Aldrin and his congregation took communion together, separated by nearly 240,000 miles, but united in the body of Christ nevertheless. Here's how Aldrin describes it in an article from Guideposts after his return:

> *I poured the wine into the chalice our church had given me. In the one-sixth gravity of the moon, the wine curled slowly and gracefully up the side of the cup. It was interesting to think that the very first liquid ever poured on the moon, and the first food eaten there, were communion elements. And so, just before I partook of the elements, I read the words which I had chosen to indicate our trust that as man probes into space we are in fact acting in Christ. I sensed especially strongly my unity with our church back home and with the Church everywhere. I read: "I am the vine, you are the branches. Whoever remains in me, and I in him, will bear much fruit; for you can do nothing without me."*[87]

---

[85] Lunar Module (LM) pilot – the technical name for the landing craft. This LM was named "Eagle," giving rise to the phrase "The Eagle has landed."

[86] National Aeronautic and Space Administration, "Apollo 11 - Technical Air-To-Ground Voice Transmission Transcription." NASA HQ. https://www.hq.nasa.gov/alsj/a11/a11transcript_tec.html. [Search on: 04 09 25 38 LMP (TRANQ)]

[87] Eugene "Buzz" Aldrin, "Guideposts Classics: Buzz Aldrin on Communion in Space." *Guideposts*, July 10, 2014, https://www.guideposts.org/better-living/life-advice/finding-life-purpose/guideposts-classics-buzz-aldrin-on-communion-in-space?nopaging=1.

Truly, that was an out-of-this-world communion experience. But communion is always an out-of-this-world experience, especially as we recognize that every time we meet at this table, we meet not only those present physically, but everyone who has ever taken communion and everyone who ever will take communion. This table connects us across miles, across denominations, across time. In I Corinthians, Paul reminds the church that there are many kinds of physical bodies, of plants, of animals, of planets and stars, and despite the differences among them, they are all connected by God's Spirit. You see, we experience a foretaste of the banquet of heaven at the communion table – a very small piece of resurrection life. Like the depths of the sea and like the multitude of stars above, the full and complete story of life-after-resurrection is still unknown.

Nevertheless, Paul tries hard to describe something of it – but one of the nuances of his point gets mangled in translation. In verse 44, Paul describes two types of bodies, or *soma* in Greek – *soma psychikon*[88] and *soma pneumatikon*.[89] Most English translations agree that *soma pneumatikon* means "spiritual bodies" – *pneuma* is the word for Spirit and breath. But where they struggle is in translating *soma psychikon*. *Psyche* means mind or soul or consciousness; think "psychology." If Paul meant "physical bodies," he would have written *soma physikon*. So, what's going on here? It seems, despite the insistence of English translations, that Paul is not contrasting *physical bodies* with *spiritual bodies*. Instead, he is saying that after the resurrection, our individual bodies will be transformed and filled with God's Holy Spirit. That, though we are separated from God and each other in our mortal bodies, the new and eternal life to come will reconnect us with God's one Spirit. How this works? We have no idea as yet. But, again, when we commune together at God's table, we experience the briefest glimpse of our spiritual bodies to come. Every communion we participate in, then, is an out-of-this-world communion, whether we celebrate here on this earthly globe, or in the depths of the sea, or on the moon and space beyond. For God's glory and majesty fill the earth and the space above, as well as the space within.

May you know that God abides in you and you in God. May you reach out to others as Christ did, seeing and loving God's image in all you encounter. And may you experience the Holy Spirit filling you and connecting you with all who are, all who have been, and all who will be. Amen.

---

[88] σῶμα ψυχικόν (soma psychikon)

[89] σῶμα πνευματικόν (soma pneumatikon)

Sending the Body of Christ into the World

Agape
(Rev. Lucus Keppel)
Matthew 15: 10-12, 15-28; Ephesians 6: 10-20

Picture this: The apostle Paul, chained to a Roman soldier on guard duty while under house arrest. He's not allowed to leave the house, wander around the capital city of Rome, and especially not allowed to go to meeting houses of the Jewish population. He's stuck inside for about four years in total, reliant on the written word alone to carry his message as far afield as he can. It's not surprising, then, that he used that time to write at least four major letters that we have preserved in the Bible today – the so-called "Prison Epistles" of Ephesians, Philippians, Colossians and Philemon.

But, as you might imagine, it can be tricky to be inspired, even when you're Paul. There's only so much to see, so much to read, so much to take in when you're chained and under house arrest, waiting on Emperor Nero to hear your case. And so, you can imagine as Paul is dictating his letter to the Ephesians that his eye falls upon his guard, and the armor he wears.

Aha! An idea!

> *Now, a final word… put on every piece of God's armor so you will be able to resist the enemy in the time of evil…. Put on the belt of Truth… the body armor of God's Righteousness…. For shoes, put on the Peace that comes from the Good News…. Hold up the shield of Faith… receive the helmet of Salvation and take the sword of the Spirit*[90]

It's a neat depiction of spiritual readiness – when under attack from evil, these are the things that protect you. And if you know a bit about how the ancient world worked, it gets even a bit cooler. The very first thing that Paul mentions is the belt of Truth – this is something of a euphemistic translation, as the Greek literally reads, "fasten around your waist with truth." Waist, in this case, doesn't mean around the hips, where we wear belts today – the Roman belt went just under the rib cage, and provided protection to your vital organs, the spleen and liver, as well as holding long straps that protected your front. But, the belt would not normally have been put on first – yet, it would likely have been noticed first! Additionally, the Greeks and Romans believed that your life and feelings were located in your liver and spleen. A military

---

[90] Ephesians 6:10-20

belt protects these vital organs – so, Paul is saying that to protect your feelings, to protect your very life energy, the best defense is truth.

The body armor – or breastplate – of God's righteousness is next. The torso armor was either chain mail or overlapping bands of metal that secured in the front. Underneath it, of course, is the heart – which the ancients believed was the seat of thought. So, Paul is saying that the best defense of your thoughts is righteousness, meaning justice coupled with mercy.

Next, Paul sees the sandals of the good news of peace. Sandals were important equipment – they allowed the ancients to walk in areas that they couldn't otherwise tread, just as shoes do for us today. The good news of peace carries you into difficult places and allows you to stand.

In addition to wearing these armor pieces, your primary defense is the shield of faith. Paul specifically mentions that this shield is able to stop the "fiery arrows of the Evil One." Faith, as Paul has said elsewhere, is a gift of God. Our work is not to make faith for ourselves, but to hold up the shield of faith in the way of evil and prevent its fires from raging.

Two more pieces – stay with me! "Receive the helmet of salvation." There are two interesting things to note in this short description – first, that the head was classically the seat of the soul – thus, "the eyes are the window to the soul." Second, instead of telling us to take up the helmet, Paul says to *receive* it, presumably from God. Paul is pointing out that your soul is protected specifically by God's action, and not your own.

Lastly, "receive the sword of the Spirit, which is the word of God." Everything so far has been for defense against an attack – left for last is the counter. Again, it is received from God – and in this case, it is the words that God has spoken which are to be the defeat of the Evil One. Note that Paul uses a different word for "word" here, *rhema*[91] – and not *logos*[92], used in John's gospel as a reference to Jesus. *Rhema* means "a word or phrase spoken" – and coupled with the fact that this is the "sword of the Spirit," it means that Paul is encouraging people to let the Spirit work through them. He even goes on to say, "Pray in the Spirit at all times and on every occasion." Prayer, not violence, are the means for Christians to defeat the schemes of evil in the world.

---

[91] ῥῆμα (rhema) – an utterance, or a thing said aloud

[92] Λόγος (logos) – Word, reason, understanding, discourse

Guard your life with truth. Protect your thoughts with justice and mercy. Prevent the spread of evil by holding onto faith. Trust that your ultimate salvation comes from God. Defeat evil by prayer and speaking God's word. That's the whole armor of God.

When evil rears its head – like it did in Charlottesville, Virginia – that's the time to put on the armor of God. When I first heard of the march there, my mouth dropped open as my newsfeed filled with image after image of protesters bearing literal torches and screaming hate-filled rhetoric. I was literally agape as I read the articles, posted as close to real time as the authors were able. Many of the protestors were wearing modern body armor and carrying plastic shields emblazoned with symbols of hatred. Counter-protesters arrived, both from local communities and from far away, and separation between the two groups was maintained not by police alone, but by members of private militia carrying assault rifles. The situation was ripe for a major clash between the protesters and anti-fascist groups, both carrying clubs and wearing armor.

How did we get here? I don't just mean recently – how can humanity have lived so long on this planet, but still not learned to love each other as fellow children of God?

In Matthew's gospel, Jesus offers a glimpse at how corruption happens. He says,

> *What goes out of the mouth comes from the heart. And that's what contaminates a person in God's sight. Out of the heart come evil thoughts, murders, adultery, prostitution, thefts, false testimonies and insults.*[93]

This is something of the opposite of the Armor of God – instead of protecting life by speaking truth, those who speak falsely contaminate themselves and those around them. Instead of upholding righteousness – justice and mercy together – those who think evil thoughts are agents of corruption and torture. Instead of withstanding the fire arrows of temptation through a shield of faith, those break vows of relationship – whether of marriage, or friendship, or family – are actively spreading fires that destroy and spread further. And so on. Jesus' point is that moral corruption is firmly rooted in humanity, and that God alone can lift us out of the spiral of corruption.

---

[93] Matthew 15: 18-19 (CEB)

Guard your life with truth. Protect your thoughts with justice and mercy. Prevent the spread of evil by holding onto faith. Trust that your ultimate salvation comes from God. Defeat evil by prayer and speaking God's word. The whole armor of God.

The very next thing that happens in the Gospel is one of the most challenging stories in the Bible. A woman whose daughter is suffering seeks out Jesus. This woman is not of Jewish heritage – Matthew says she is Canaanite, Mark that she is Syrophoenician – the point is, she's not one of Jesus' own people. And Jesus ignores her cries for help, but she keeps trying. The disciples ask Jesus to get rid of her, and he says, seemingly to the air, that he was only sent to the people of Israel. Again, she asks him for help, and he speaks again, "It is not good to take the children's bread and toss it to little dogs." She replies, "Yes, Lord. But even the dogs eat the crumbs that fall off their masters' table." And with that, Jesus replies, "Lady, you have great faith. It will be just as you wish."[94]

"Lady, you have great faith." This is the only time in all of Matthew's gospel that Jesus tells someone that their faith is great. It's also the only time in all of Scripture where Jesus loses an argument – well, except for the same story in Mark's gospel.

She's the ultimate foil to the disciples, for Matthew. Again, and again, Jesus criticizes the disciples for their lack of faith. And here she is, an outsider many times over – a foreigner, not Jewish, and a woman – yet she's the one person praised for her great faith. You can just picture the disciples with their mouths agape – perhaps, even as yours was when you heard this story for the first time. Whether Jesus was testing her, or focused solely in one place, or genuinely changed his message after meeting her, we don't know. But listen to this, from Lutheran pastor David Lose:

> *We do know that this woman did not retreat to silence, but spoke out, offering a testimony that rings down through the ages: "See me! See me as a person, not as a woman or a Canaanite or a minority or a foreigner or someone from a different religion or as a burden. See me as a person and child of God. And he did. The question before us… is whether we will.*[95]

---

[94] Matthew 15:21-28

[95] David Lose, "Pentecost 11A: The Canaanite Woman's Lesson," *Dear Partner in Preaching* (blog), August 14, 2017, http://www.davidlose.net/2017/08/pentecost-

The Canaanite woman spoke up, over the din of people proclaiming salvation for their people alone, over the silence from Jesus himself and made herself known. Though she was ignored, and dismissed, she was eventually praised for her great faith. She wore the whole armor of God, and broke down barriers, perhaps opening the way for us to see each and every other person as a child of God, worthy of love.

Among the counter-protesters in Charlottesville were religious leaders and congregants from many different denominations and faiths, who linked arms to prevent access to vulnerable people, sang hymns to drown out the nasty slogans and insults shouted by the protesters, and when a car was intentionally driven through the counter-protesters, many of the religious leaders ran towards it, to offer whatever assistance they could. That's what wearing the whole armor of God looks like in practice. Running towards danger, bearing good news of peace and wholeness, shielding others whether they shared their faith or not, trusting in God for salvation, and speaking words of righteousness and truth as the Spirit leads.

In so doing, they showed God's love and care for all in the world, not just for one group. They spoke up, like the Canaanite woman, on behalf of those whose very humanity was being questioned. Against the vitriol spewing from those filled with corruption and hatred, they put their faith in God into action and worked to heal the brokenness.

One of those people of faith made an impact, as reported by Jack Jenkins:

> *[Lisa Sharon] Harper says she did a tiny bit of [the work of justice and being in right relationship with those God hears and holds most closely] on [that] Saturday. As she stood for hours in front of a line of militia members – who were reportedly instructed not to speak to press or protestors – she says she began to wear [one of them] down. When she turned to leave to avoid increasing violence, she addressed the man one last time. 'I just want you to know, we love you,' she said. The man's face, grizzled and tired from the day, suddenly softened. After a moment, he replied: 'I love you too.'* [96]

11-a-the-canaanite-womans-lesson/.

[96] Jack Jenkins, "Meet the Clergy Who Stared down White Supremacists in Charlottesville," *ThinkProgress*, August 16, 2017, https://thinkprogress.org/clergy-in-charlottesville-e95752415c3e/.

My friends, one final thought: the Greek word for the love that God shows the world, the most perfect love, the love we can bring into the world through wearing the whole armor of God – that Greek word is *agapē*.[97] *Agapē* – spelled exactly like the word agape. Because when we find ourselves agape, it is imperative that we seek out *agapē*, standing against racism, standing against anti-Semitism, standing against any *-ism* that tries to get us to believe one person or group of people is lesser than any other group. Rev. Dr. Martin Luther King, Jr puts it best:

> *I refuse to accept the view that [humanity] is so tragically bound to the starless midnight of racism and war that the bright daybreak of peace and brotherhood can never become a reality… I believe that unarmed truth and unconditional love will have the final word.*[98]

Guard your life with truth. Protect your thoughts with justice and mercy. Prevent the spread of evil by holding onto faith. Trust that your ultimate salvation comes from God. Defeat evil by prayer and speaking God's word. Put on the whole armor of God, turning agape into *agapē*. Amen.

---

[97] ἀγάπη (agape, pron. ah-GAH-pay) from ἀγαπάω (agapao), to love.

[98] Martin Luther King, Jr., "Acceptance Speech," *Nobelprize.org*, December 10, 1964, https://www.nobelprize.org/prizes/peace/1964/king/26142-martin-luther-king-jr-acceptance-speech-1964/.

Called to Freedom
(Rev. Elana Levy)
Luke 6:27-28, 31-36; Galatians 5:13-15; I Peter 3:8-16a

As we head into Independence Day, I thought it might be interesting to look at what the Bible teaches us about freedom, how it influenced the founding fathers, and what that means for us now. July 4th was the day that the delegates met for the Second Continental Congress and adopted the Declaration of Independence. They came together to fight back against the British because they believed that they were subject to tyranny.[99]

This cause for freedom, for liberty, sprang both from the powerful impact of the Great Awakening – the religious revival that swept the nation – and from rationalism – a movement that lifted up reason as the path to truth, the strength of the mind over the privilege of wealth and class. Distaste for taxation and stricter policies from the British was widespread in the colonies and so the people came together to fight as one – for the freedom to be a new kind of nation.[100]

As we look back at the heroes of our history, it can be easy to romanticize things – to make the course of events seem easy or inevitable. But though they felt called to freedom, things were by no means certain. Of the 2.5 million people living in the colonies during the revolution, up to around 500,000 supported the British in the war. (For all you math people, that's 20% of the colonists!) And even among the patriots, many of them had more that was different from one another than they had in common. They were rich and poor, men and women, country folk and city folk, farmers and merchants, white and black. There were 9,000 free blacks who fought with

---

[99] "Second Continental Congress," in *Wikipedia: The Free Encyclopedia*, Wikimedia Foundation Inc., updated 28 August 2018, https://en.wikipedia.org/wiki/Second_Continental_Congress.

[100] "American Revolution," in *Wikipedia: The Free Encyclopedia*, Wikimedia Foundation Inc., updated 6 September 2018, https://en.wikipedia.org/wiki/American_Revolution.

the Patriots, [101] about 100 Jews,[102] and a handful of Muslims[103] who have been recorded in lists of revolutionary soldiers. And even among Christians there was rarely easy agreement. Back then, it was a lot more common to believe that people who were not the same denomination as you were doomed to hell. And yet, the Declaration was adopted and signed by Episcopalians, Congregationalists, Presbyterians, Quakers, Unitarians, Deists, and one Catholic.[104] Even today it's hard to imagine what that group would perfectly agree on…

I'll stop with the details. I'm going a long way to make a short point: the people who fought for our freedom rose above just about every division imaginable in their day to do what they thought was right. In different ways, with different roles and focuses, they came together despite class, wealth, gender, race, religion, place of origin, and on and on.

Freedom means that all of us have the right to make our own choices: to worship, to speak, to live, to pursue happiness as we see fit. In Galatians, we find Paul talking about freedom, but he's talking very specifically about freedom in Christ. Paul says that freedom in Christ means salvation comes by grace through faith in Christ. That means that you don't have to worry about whose interpretations of the laws you follow – loose or strict – as long as your choices don't interfere with salvation, he taught that you could do (or not do) anything you want.

And that's the key, right? As Christians living in freedom, we know that we are sinners, but we also know that doesn't give us permission to go set fire to a library or taunt school children just 'cause we feel like it. In Galatians, Paul tells us, "You were called to freedom, brothers and sisters; only do not use your freedom as an opportunity for self-indulgence, but through love become slaves to one another." Now, isn't that something else? The Bible says that freedom isn't for freedom for its own sake. And right after Paul says we are

---

[101] Ibid.

[102] Norman H. Finkelstein, "The Revolutionary War and the Jews," *My Jewish Learning*, 2012-2018, https://www.myjewishlearning.com/article/the-revolutionary-war-and-the-jews/.

[103] "Muslims in the United States Military," in *Wikipedia: The Free Encyclopedia*, Wikimedia Foundation Inc., updated 6 September 2018 https://en.wikipedia.org/wiki/Muslims_in_the_United_States_military.

[104] "Religious Affiliation of the Founding Fathers of the United States of America," *Adherents*, 2013, http://www.adherents.com/gov/Founding_Fathers_Religion.html.

called to freedom, he says – you're free so go be slaves to one another through love. The irony there is not accidental. This word for freedom is the same word used for a slave liberated from slavery. And here he goes, telling us to be slaves through *agape* – slaves through the love that God loves us with, the love that we show when we try to live by God's will for humanity.

When I think about the founding fathers and everything they rose above to form common cause, I wonder in silence. For them, the enemy was tyranny, the enemy was any who would take away the rights of another (thankfully, our sense of who is worthy of human rights has improved since then). Still, we built on their ideals and courage to become a society united in these freedoms. Jesus told us to love our enemies – he knew that we'd always manage to find enemies for ourselves. And I think of America now as I ponder the question: "Who is our enemy?"

Most of us could point to a few countries on the map who mean us harm or international terrorist groups with foul, inhuman plots. And, well, if you define an enemy as someone who is openly hostile, acting from a deep-seated hatred, then I'd say those are certainly enemies. But if we watch the news, hear the pundits, scan our Facebook feeds, overhear strangers in coffee shops, it seems like we spend more and more of our energy making enemies of our fellow Americans. We don't seem to talk to each other much anymore – we talk at each other or, worse, we only talk to our "side." We form political camps, camps of Christian versus Christian, age-based camps, gender-based, sports -based – it seems like any possible difference we have any more, we're drawing thicker lines and more menacing boundaries. Any who disagree or even appear to be on the other side are quickly barraged with insults, anger, impatience. Their motives and intelligence are immediately suspect, and we mock and sneer as we shut down conversation so often; too often.

Jesus said, "Love your enemies." Have we come to that as a nation, as people of faith? Are we so deeply washed in the values of our own side (whatever it is) that we cannot believe that a stranger has values, too? Are we so proud that we claim that we could never make a mistake or learn from another? Is it so easy to act mean-spirited that we don't care who we hurt anymore?

Paul's voice rings out, echoing Jesus, echoing Leviticus:

> *The whole law is summed up in a single commandment, 'You shall love your neighbor as yourself.' If, however, you bite and devour one another, take care that you are not consumed by one another.*[105]

If we have to attack anyone with a different idea from our own, we won't have to worry about our foreign enemies – we'll destroy each other ourselves. If the founding fathers spoke to each other like we do and treated each other like we do, we might still be subjects of the British Empire!

Friends, as Christians, we are called to spend each day of our lives trying to be more like Jesus. And Jesus did not bite and devour those who moved against him. When he reached out for hearts to guide and to heal, he crossed all the barriers and divisions of his day. To those who stood against him, he offered prayer, forgiveness, forbearance, and patient love. The heart of our lives, our holy savior bids us see that he stands more powerful than any division we imagine or create on earth. If we wish to give ourselves to him, we must hear his call to celebrate his holy name over all other voices that would lead us to quarrel with and despise our neighbor.

In Christ, we are free – this is our great responsibility. Giving thanks for that freedom, we can act in ways that glorify God, that love our neighbors, that feed the soul. Where we sin, we can engage in the freedom to be made anew when we repent and confess our sins. It is because we are truly free that scripture so often appeals to the goodness in us – to get up, to keep trying, to seek the good, to do good once more. Peter tells us, "Finally, all of you, have unity of spirit, sympathy, love for one another, a tender heart, and a humble mind. Do not repay evil for evil or abuse for abuse; but…repay with a blessing."

And so, let us choose to use our freedom for unity, for love, for tender hearts, and humble minds. Let us speak words of kindness and blessing to all we meet in person or online. As people of faith, we know what God has done for us in Christ Jesus. We know what promise, what grace, what life lies before us. So, may we learn from Jesus and Paul and Peter and speak of the hope that rests in our hearts, with gentleness and with reverence. Amen.

---

[105] Galatians 5:14-15

Connecting with the Spirit
(Rev. Lucus Keppel)
John 5:1-9a; Acts 8: 4-25

On the way back from a Presbytery meeting in Las Cruces, New Mexico, Elana and I passed a billboard advertising a church in Alamogordo. Perhaps you've seen this sign, or one like it - it read, "Relationship - not religion." Elana and I both pulled a face, and of course, kept driving. But you see, for so many people, even the word "religion" is a pejorative, a word used to describe and dismiss the spiritual practices of others. Now, I'm not dismissing that a relationship with God is important - far from it - but I think we need to talk about what religion is, and why it is NOT a bad word. Religion comes originally from Latin - *Religare* - which meant to bind together. Later, it became *Religio* - obligation, bond, or reverent observation, and then in Middle English, Religion, meaning "life under vows". One could have a faith of one's own - but in religion, you were bound to a code that you either chose for yourself, or that you felt God had led you to. There's a fine point here: you choose to be bound by the vows you make and are not forced into the choice. Yes, it did occasionally happen that people were forced by their family or circumstance into the monastery or convent - but usually, it was something chosen for yourself. A spiritual practice of restriction - a lot like what people today may do during the season of Lent.

You have likely heard the phrase, "Spiritual, but not Religious". The sense in this is that one can be connected to the Spirit of God without being bound into one religious track. And true - the Spirit of God does work in and through people that we find surprising choices, but this phrase too dismisses religion as something that holds you back. Yet, if that's the case, why would anyone choose voluntarily to be religious? To join in the dance of the universe, you must give up everything that is not the right step at the right time. Or, as the Renaissance artist Michelangelo is reported to have said, you must remove everything from the block of marble that is not the beautiful sculpture inside.

Maybe you've heard of the 20th Century monk Thomas Merton, a man who gave up a loving relationship to take vows as a Trappist monk in Kentucky. He chose to take on additional religious activities in order to become closer with God. Merton believed that we live in a world that is absolutely transparent, and God shines through it all the time - in people and in things and in nature and in events. But we don't see it. We need to remember to see. We need to seek not to know ABOUT God - but to seek to KNOW God. That direct, personal experience.

For everyone, that direct personal experience of God is found through spiritual practice. Prayer is a spiritual practice. So is Yoga. So is walking through the woods, or along the fence line, and appreciating God's hand in the world. So is the acceptance of additional burdens - like the vows of monks and nuns - or the choice not to curse, or to remove your hat in church - or to PUT ON a hat in worship! Spiritual practice is everywhere - and it is the root of religion. To claim that you can have a relationship without religion is nonsensical in the extreme. Think of relationships you have had - every single one of them involves compromise, involves voluntary restrictions of one sort or another, hopefully to the benefit of you both. It is the same with the relationship with God - you take on voluntary obligations to strengthen your ties with the Divine - and it ought to spill over into strengthening your ties with your fellow human beings.

The scriptures are full of this sense of religion as voluntary restriction. From the Nazarite vows, like Samson took, to the Pharisees choosing movement restrictions, and even the disciples leaving everything behind to follow Jesus, it can seem like religion is all about giving up something. But - it's a choice of giving something up that was distracting you from seeing the Divine in all things. In the Gospel of John, we learn of a man who, for thirty-eight years, sat by the pool at Bethesda (or Bethzetha) in Jerusalem, waiting for it to bubble and stir - and try to be the first in the water. Day after day, for 38 years, trying to make it in before anyone else, and yet being unable to make it, due to his paralyzed legs. Jesus comes up to him, and asks him simply, "Do you want to be healed?" Does he want to be healed? For 38 years, he's been trying! And he's nearly given up hope - he says, "I cannot walk, and if I am going to make it into the pool first, I need someone to carry me. Someone beats me there every time." For him, it has become a matter of life-long faith that one day, someone will carry him in to the water. His spiritual practice is to wait for that time to come - actively wait, asking passersby to help him in. And finally, he's asked the right person - not to help him into the water, but to heal him, his actual goal! Jesus doesn't lay hands on him, doesn't do anything other than tell him to stand up, pick up his mat, and walk. And just like that, 38 years of waiting by the pool's edge come to an end. He doesn't stop to ask who Jesus is, he just picks up his mat, and walks away - probably filled with joy![106]

In Acts, similarly, we learn of a man named Simon who has converted to believing in Jesus. He was a magician, and people thought he was possibly the Messiah, given all the things he could make happen. Oddly, we know of

---

[106] John 5:1-9a

Simon from three different texts of the first Century - he's an actual historical figure of note! But though he had begun to believe in Jesus after seeing Philip perform miracles, he didn't quite get it - he didn't quite give up those things that were separating him from seeing God at work in the world. So when John and Peter show up, and people start responding to the Holy Spirit at work in them, Simon thinks that this is a trick like those he used to do. So, he asks to buy the knowledge of passing on the Holy Spirit through laying-on-of-hands from Peter and John - and Peter tells him off.

> *"May your money tarnish and rot away, you who think to buy God's power! Give up this way of thinking - repent of your wickedness - and pray for God's forgiveness, and that God transforms your heart."*[107]

For this, we get the concept of *simony* - trying to buy church office or spiritual power. Simon needed to give up his conception of how the world worked in order to become close enough with the Divine to see the Holy Spirit at work in the world. Simon had a relationship with Philip - and through Philip, Jesus - but hadn't quite gotten the religion part together. Simon wants to lead in the dance with God and the universe but hadn't learned the steps. Hadn't listened to the rhythm. Yet, after this admonishment, he asks Peter to pray on his behalf, that he might change his ways - Simon wants to change! The text leaves him there, but I think the implication is that Simon worked to change his heart and acted out of love - and joined the dance with God.

So, how do you connect with the Spirit of God? Most Presbyterians, when asked this question, will respond at least partially with "Prayer". Now, in our Directory for Worship - part of the constitution of the Presbyterian Church (USA), prayer is defined as:

> *A gift from God, who desires dialogue and relationship with us. It is a posture of faith and a way of living in the world. Prayer is also the primary way we participate in worship... There are many kinds of prayer – adoration, thanksgiving, confession, supplication, intercession, dedication. There are many ways to pray – listening and waiting for God, remembering God's gracious acts, crying out to God for help, or offering oneself to God. Prayer may be spoken, silent, sung, or enacted in physical ways.*[108]

---

[107] Acts 8:4-24

[108] "Directory for Worship," in *Book of Order*, W-2.0202, Vol. 2. The Constitution of the Presbyterian Church (USA) (Louisville: Westminster Press, 2016), 84.

Or, as it's so delightfully put by a friend of John Phillip Newell:

> *There are two types of prayer: One is the dozing kitten prayer, purring by the warm fire of God's presence. The other is the yappy dog prayer, scratching at the door of heaven, imploring God's help in our lives.*[109]

We focus a LOT of effort on the yappy-dog prayer - trying to choose the right words, thinking that if we just pull the right phrase from the air, God will do what we *want*. Yet, if we focus more on the dozing kitten prayer - "listening in silence, an expectancy" as Merton puts it - we might be able to hear where God is leading us to what we *need*. John Philip Newell writes:

> *Spiritual practice is not about self-important seriousness. Rather, it is about doing something that... is both less serious and more serious - a Cosmic Dance in which we discover that we do not have to take the lead. We cannot take the lead, for we do not know how to. But we can give ourselves to the Dance. We can let go with abandon to it, to be carried by its endless rhythm in a relationship that is deeper than our consciousness can comprehend. But what is most serious about the dance is that each one of us is needed. There is a place in the dance of the universe that no one else can take but each of us.*[110]

Religion is about learning the steps to the Cosmic Dance - giving up of the things that distract us from the rhythm, that prevent us from seeing God's shining light in the world. To connect with the Spirit, we need to listen more - to seek the rhythm and move with God and each other.

May God bless your dancing, that you may bless others. May Christ lead your steps, that you may not stumble. May your spirit be caught up in the Holy Spirit, until you see nothing but the light of God, hear nothing but the rhythm of Christ, and feel nothing but the love of the Holy Spirit. Amen.

---

[109] John Philip Newell, "Reconnecting with Spiritual Practice." In *The Rebirthing of God: Christianity's Struggle for New Beginnings* (Woodstock: Christian Journeys, 2014), 67.

[110] Ibid, 70.

The Treasure of Dunkin' John
(Rev. Lucus Keppel)
Mark 1:1-8; Isaiah 40:1-11

How many stories, movies, and video games involve a story of seeking a hidden treasure? I can think of many just off hand – the *Goonies, Treasure Island, Assassin's Creed: Black Flag, Peter Pan, The Secret of Monkey Island* – and that's just the ones related to pirate treasure! Throw in the Dan Brown books and movies, half of everything starring Nicholas Cage, and all of the *Final Fantasy* games, and you're already to overload. Needless to say, it's a pretty popular trope. And, as we are traveling through Advent, let's become Advent-urers, and look at the scripture lessons for today in a new light – a treasure map around well-traveled waters and landmarks we may never see the same way again.

Are you ready, Advent-urers? Close your eyes for a moment. It's dark outside, and the map we have before us is lit only by an oil lamp, enclosed in glass. Hesitantly, we sound out the first line of writing: *"Arche tou euaggeliou 'Iesou Christou uiou Theou."*[111] Open your eyes, my friends - that's the beginning of the Gospel of Mark in Koine Greek. Since Mark was the first written Gospel, that means that that is also the first that many people heard of the story of Jesus Christ, son of God – *'Iesou Christou uiou theou*. It's a beautiful, short description of what's to follow – beginning at the beginning, *arche* (like archaic) and then using a word that literally means "good message," *euaggeliou*. If that sounds a little familiar, you're right! English borrowed it from a Latinized version – from *euaggeliou* to *evangelion* to evangelism. Well, sort of. It's a noun, so it would be closer if we had a word "evangel" in English, meaning "the thing that is evangelized".

Arche tou euaggeliou 'Iesou Christou uiou theou. The beginning of the evangel – (or good message) of Jesus Christ, son of God. Our treasure map is pointing us to the message of Jesus. What is this message? Mark spends the rest of his book telling us one step after another and leaves us hanging with the instruction to go to Galilee – but that's a sermon for another time. We're not at the end – we're at the beginning of our journey!

So, let's go back to our map, lit by lamplight. We're holding the treasure map before us – a map to the good message of Jesus Christ. And after the

---

[111] Ἀρχὴ τοῦ εὐαγγελίου Ἰησοῦ Χριστοῦ υἱοῦ θεοῦ. (Arche tou euaggeliou 'Iesou Christou uiou Theou)

introduction sentence, the first thing that Mark does is... quote scripture. "Look, I am sending my messenger before you – he will prepare your way, a voice shouting in the wilderness: "Prepare the way of the Lord; make his paths straight."" Ancient prophesy, which Mark attributes to Isaiah. Ooh, this gives us a place to start! To understand the good message, we need to look at the prophecies and scriptures! Mark is telling us that this map is not the actual beginning, but part of a longer story. Now, should you want to read through the Old Testament before we continue, you're welcome to do so – just mark the book here and return when you're ready!

Ah, good – most of you are still with me! You're aware, then, that though Mark attributes Isaiah with this prophesy, he's actually cobbled it together in what scholars rather generously call "a composite quotation". He's mixed verses from Exodus, Malachi, and Isaiah – not something we today think is a good way of using scripture, but his standards were different. That's ok. We see that he is very familiar with scripture, to throw it together like this – and he expects us to be, too.

So, what is the Isaiah passage describing, since Mark directs our attention to it so intentionally? It, too, is a new beginning. Having been in captivity in Babylon for decades, at last, the people of Judah are to head home! God calls out to the people to take comfort, all of them, from the richest to the poorest, for their time of suffering is over, and the way is being made clear to go home. Some messengers are skeptical of this message – after all, humanity is still just as weak as before, just as perishable as grass – but God tells the messenger that God is mighty enough to make up for our weakness. "Here is the Lord God, coming with strength, with a triumphant arm, bringing reward and payment." Strength, triumphant arm, dispensing reward and payment – this is an image of a warrior-king, arriving to lead the people. But when this mighty one arrives, how does God use God's strength? Not to destroy, not to harm, but to gather the scattered lamps into God's arms, to lift them into God's lap, to "gently guide the nursing ewes." In other words, the arrival of God shows the strength of peace, and the loving nature of the Holy One. Don't be afraid to speak of God's true nature, Isaiah shouts to us – for God is powerfully peaceful, and God guides us with a gentle hand, back to our true home, even if we have been away for seventy or eighty years.

Mapmaker Mark uses this Isaiah reference to remind us of that experience of wonder at God's true nature, and point us on the trajectory of the treasure of Jesus Christ. Now, Mark takes us to his first character, usually named "John the Baptist." That's a fine translation of his name – traditional, solid – but since we're looking for a more "treasure hunting" flavor, let's look more closely. "There appeared *Io'annes 'o Baptizon*[112] in the wilderness..." *Ioannes* is the Greek pronunciation of the Hebrew *Yehohanan*, meaning "the Holy One is Gracious." *Baptizo* in Greek means to immerse – or, more colloquially, to dunk. *Yehohanan* the Immerser – or Dunkin' John, the Wildman. He has been wearing scratchy, rough clothes made of camel's hair, eating only the most simple of foods that he can find in the desert wilderness, and calling people to change their ways. Dunkin' John is a pretty scary fella, all told - wild in appearance and in manner. Yet, he is a prophet of God, calling people to change their hearts and lives, as they ask God to forgive their sin.

In his wildness, he is perceived as God's holy instrument, a holy prophet who has forsaken easy living in the village and city for a connection with the divine. His difficult circumstances, it was believed, allowed him the opportunity to speak with God, and interpret God's desires. Yet, this crazy-looking Dunkin' John, seen as holy in his wildness, claimed that he was only a messenger, pointing the way to someone stronger. "I immerse you in water, but he will immerse you in the Holy Spirit."

Here, adventurers, is the first landmark of our Markan Treasure Map – Dunkin' John, pointing to someone who will come to immerse everyone in the Holy Spirit. People flocked to Dunkin' John not because they wanted a bath, but because they had already decided to ask forgiveness. You see, this landmark of ours isn't only known through the Bible. Dunkin' John was famous enough to be written about by historians of the day – and here's what Josephus the historian has to say about him:

> *[He] exhorted the Jews to lead righteous lives, to practice justice towards their fellows and piety towards God, and so doing, to join in baptism. In his view this was a necessary preliminary if baptism was to be acceptable to God. They must not employ it to gain pardon for whatever sins they committed, but as a consecration of the body implying that the soul was already cleansed by right behavior.*[113]

Like any good mapmaker, then, Mark has pointed us to a very visible landmark, and tied into the grand story of God's action in the world through scripture. The map tells us of the treasure: the good message of Jesus Christ,

---

[112] Ἰωάνης ὁ βαπτίζων (ioanes o baptizon)

[113] Josephus, *Jewish Antiquities*, 18.117, in *Mark*, by Alan Culpepper, Vol. 20, Smyth Smyth & Helwys Bible Commentary (Macon: Smyth & Helwys Publishing, 2007), 47.

God's Son. It tells us where the treasure comes from: the scriptures that point to God's action in the world, of the powerful peace that God brings. It tells us the first landmark pointing our way: Dunkin' John, who acted to recognize the changed hearts and changed actions of the people of Judea. And it tells us that everything that John is doing merely makes the way clear for the Holy One to come, who will not only recognize right action on the outside, through immersion in water, but will immerse us in the very being of God, in the Holy Spirit. What does this mean, but to be gathered up in God's arms, to be truly part of God's powerful peacemaking action.

There is much of the treasure map to be explored, fellow adventurers, and we will continue through Mark's map for the rest of this year, even after the season of advent has ended. But I urge you, however long you've been seeking the treasure of Dunkin' John, the good message of Jesus Christ, not to give up hope. Whether decades or centuries pass, whether the world has ever seemed darker, hold on to your hope for peace, the powerful peace that God brings. For God already has gathered you into God's arms, and is guiding you home.

May you lean into God's arms, being supported by God's powerful peace. May your search for the good message of Jesus lead you to act rightly, a true follower of his Way. And may you always be immersed in the Holy Spirit, that whenever you start to wander from the way, the valleys will be lifted up, and the mountains made low, to bring you back to God's fold. Amen.

Homelight
(Rev. Lucus Keppel)
Matthew 2:1-12; Isaiah 60:1-6

It is cold this year, my friends – cold enough throughout the east coast that Floridians are experiencing snow, parts of Boston flooded and froze, and the Niagara Falls are a solid mass of icicles. On Lake Michigan, the St. Joseph lighthouse has been covered with layer after layer of ice as the spray from the lake coats it and freezes in place – and yet, the beacon still shines from its housing. I was struck by how incredibly powerful this image was: a lighthouse, designed to shine a bright light into the night so that others could find their way, still doing its job despite layers and layers of buildup in a frozen world.

God is like this, too: shining a light into the world to be picked up and reflected by each of us, even through the crud that covers us. Yes, on Epiphany Sunday, we're talking about the light that guided the Magi to Jesus – but we're also talking about the light that guided the Israelites back to their homeland, and the light that guides us home to God every day.

In the midst of the exile in Babylon, the people of Israel and Judah could hardly have thought that they would make it home. So, when the writer in the Isaiah tradition announced to the people in exile that their light had come, and the Lord's glory shone around them, this had to be baffling. True, the Neo-Babylonian Empire had just been overcome by the Persian Empire, but that just meant that there was a change in who was in control, right? No, says the Prophet: you are still in the control of God, whom you have served even in exile from your homeland. And God is calling you to look up – to shine out God's light into the dark and gloomy world as a beacon to call you home – and also all of God's other children throughout the world.

What great hope it would have been to hear these words:

> *Lift up your eyes and look all around: they are all gathered; they have come to you. Your sons will come from far away, and your daughters on caregivers' hips. Then you will see and be radiant; your heart will tremble and open wide.* [114]

Even when things are at their worst, God calls to the people to be beacons in the night, bearers of God's own glory that bursts forth from open hearts. How wonderful for those who heard these words, and had their hearts

---

[114] Isaiah 60:4-5a (CEB)

opened, that Cyrus the Great of Persia returned the Jewish people to their homeland! The light of God shone from an unexpected place in that time – from the height of Empire, a restoration was received.

And what a restoration! Not only were the exiled returned home, but trade resumed, and foreigners came to honor and worship God. It seems that, even in exile, the light that shown through the Jewish people was enough to guide others to God's faith. When Isaiah promises that "countless camels will cover your land, from Midian and Ephah and Sheba,"[115] he is saying that these people from near and far will come back, too. Midian and Ephah are thought to be on the Arabian Peninsula – either confederations of nomadic tribes or just Hebraic names for the tribes themselves. Sheba probably refers to people living in modern-day Ethiopia, Eritrea, and Yemen who were linked to the Jews through the child of Solomon with the Queen of Sheba. The mention of camels suggests trade, especially when linked with frankincense, a major trade good of the Arabian Peninsula – and the modern archeological evidence suggests that the Sheban people had set up a series of trade posts and ports along the Arabian sea and Nile. In any case, the point is that the return home wasn't to a miserable existence, but rather, to an abundance that would build over time.

That brings us to Matthew's story of the Magi – the learned ones who studied the heavens and were often called on for divination in the Persian world. The Magi of Matthew's day were likely from the Parthian Empire, outside the Roman sphere of influence. The Parthians and the Romans had been fighting for over fifty years when Jesus was born – and would continue to struggle against each other for six hundred more years, the longest continuous war in human history, leaving both empires crippled and ultimately vulnerable to the rise of the Caliphate. Needless to say, the Magi would have been looked on with suspicion by the Roman authorities, and even a client king, like Herod the Great, would have distrusted the Parthians. Yet, because of the historical connections between the Persians and the Jews, the Magi would have been well received by most Jewish people.

It makes a certain amount of sense, then, for these Magi to have seen the star, interpreted it according to their way, and followed it to find a newborn king. It makes a lot less sense for them to visit with the current client-king. Herod cannot claim to be *born* as "King of the Jews", since he was not of Jewish descent himself. Matthew takes a certain amount of glee in pointing this out, too – for Herod has to ask his staff about the scriptures, instead of

---

[115] Isaiah 60:6 (CEB)

knowing them for himself. Yet, he directs the Magi to the right place, and they bring Jesus gifts fit for a king, returning home by another route after God warns them not to go back to Herod. [116]

Though the Magi were first guided by the light of the star, they also saw the light of Christ and were guided by his light to return to their home. Whatever spark of divine connection led them to Christ, you can bet that the light of their encounter shone through them thereafter. God's light shines through the strangest of places, like the light of that lighthouse shining through the frozen spray. That light led the Magi on their path, and the light that Christ shines ought to lead us on our path, too.

My friends, you have a light – or rather, THE light – inside of you. Whether it is but a single coal that the Spirit occasionally moves by and flares up, or a lighthouse beacon that shines any direction you look, that light is the love of God shining from you. And like the light of the Christmas star, which called to people far afield at its rising, the light of God's love in you also calls to people far afield. When we confess in a moment that Christ is light from light, we are affirming our faith in Christ's light, still shining in the world today, still guiding us home. God is our *homelight*, and we are called to respond to God's light with brilliant actions of our own.

Let's conclude with this beautiful prayer:

Stars that shine above
Tell of God's love -
For even when clouds hide,
Still, they are there.
So we, dear Father,
Though Shadows hide Thee,
Know Thou art keeping watch
With tenderest care. Amen.[117]

---

[116] Matthew 2:1-12

[117] "Stars That Shine Above," poem by Charles John Keppel, First United Community Church, Detroit, MI. Great-Grandfather of Lucus.

Index

Abuse..............107, 108, 110, 146

Aldrin, Eugene.................131, 133

America............99, 102, 128, 145

Angels..................... 40, 56, 79, 152

Anger...........36, 37, 38, 56, 145

    as fire 36, 38

    as warning light.................37

Armstrong, Neil...............131, 133

Bablyon .. 41, 42, 61, 73, 128, 152, 155

Babylon 23, 41, 155

Baptism .. 118, 119, 120, 121, 130, 153

    water of 153, 154

Bible..... 27, 36, 40, 62, 67, 68, 69, 70, 83, 91, 93, 109, 110, 119, 125, 127, 137, 140, 143, 145, 153

Bible Citations

    Isaiah 40 28

    Proverbs 17 51

Brown, Alton............................ 122

Brown, Dan............................... 151

Calvin, John 120

Camping.........................56, 61, 89

Canaan....................... 140, 141

Canada..74

Christians 52, 68, 90, 109, 111, 118, 124, 139, 144, 145, 146

Collins, Michael........................ 131

Comfort.. 27, 28, 61, 85, 112, 119, 128, 152

Communion 31, 122, 128, 130, 133

    bread of 122, 124, 125, 126, 127, 130, 133

Confessions of the Church

    Brief Statement of Faith...30

    Heidelberg Catechism.......28

    Scots Confession 30

Dancing 29, 30, 31, 113, 147, 149, 150

Darkness 23, 24, 55, 56, 112, 120, 155

Death...... 27, 55, 95, 96, 110, 111, 112, 113

Debt....37, 99, 100, 101, 102, 103, 111, 124

Egypt 50, 68, 109, 120, 156

Europe..74

    England........... 124, 143, 146

    Germany 124

    Spain 35

Evil......23, 25, 26, 38, 52, 57, 100, 110, 137, 138, 139, 140, 142, 146

Faith 23, 24, 26, 38, 41, 43, 49, 51, 53, 57, 70, 81, 91, 109, 110, 111, 112, 113, 123, 124, 137, 138, 139, 140, 141, 142, 144, 145, 146, 147, 148, 149, 156, 157

    loss of 37

Family...26, 41, 48, 49, 55, 56, 68, 72, 73, 80, 81, 82, 83, 84, 85, 98, 108, 112, 120, 122, 139, 147

    children 24, 35, 47, 48, 70, 73, 74, 79, 81, 82, 83, 84, 85,

109, 118, 120, 121, 132, 140, 144

Fear 23, 57, 69, 73, 81, 92, 99, 108, 109, 119, 130, 132

Fire. 43, 51, 52, 53, 61, 62, 63, 89, 90

Forgiveness 51, 56, 62, 69, 100, 103, 146, 149, 153

    reconciliation 103, 130

Freedom 38, 41, 47, 48, 69, 73, 99, 100, 101, 114, 143, 144, 146

    independence . 127, 128, 143

    of conscience 41

Galilee 79, 97

Glory 23, 26, 132, 134, 146, 155

God 23, 24, 26, 27, 31, 37, 38, 40, 41, 42, 49, 52, 53, 55, 57, 62, 63, 68, 69, 70, 73, 74, 75, 81, 82, 85, 91, 94, 95, 98, 100, 109, 110, 113, 118, 119, 120, 122, 123, 124, 125, 127, 128, 130, 132, 134, 138, 139, 140, 141, 142, 145, 146, 147, 148, 149, 150, 155

    action of 51, 52, 138, 147, 149, 153, 154

    armor of .. 137, 139, 140, 141

    armor of God 139

    arms of 152, 154

    as mother 83, 84

    calling of 68

    children of 49

    fingers of 132

    forgiveness of .... *See* Forgiveness

    glory of 91, 113, 155, *See* Glory

    grace of 28, 29, 30, 31, 53, 54, 73, 123, 130, 144, 146

    heart of 52

    image of 36, 92

    kingdom of *See* Heaven: kingdom of

    light of 23, 121, 147, 150, 155, 156, 157

    love of 27, 28, 29, 30, 31, 49, 74, 141, 152, 157

    nature of 152

    order of 132

    peace of 154

    power of 49, 95, 125, *See* Power

    presence of . 40, 42, 129, 150

    righteousness of 36

    sovereignty of 27, 28, 29, 30, 31, 155

    strength of 23

    word of 138

    wrath of 30, 36

Gold 50, 51, 52, 118

Goodness ... 23, 24, 31, 37, 38, 53, 56, 57, 63, 72, 82, 85, 91, 97, 108, 109, 111, 122, 123, 126, 128, 140, 146, 153, 154

Gospel 55, 74, 94, 95, 109, 110, 112, 119, 126, 137, 138, 140, 141

Gratitude 62, 63, 133, 146

Greece 50, 100, 101, 125, 128

Grief....... 55, 56, 82, 94, 111, 112, 113

Healing..... 38, 56, 62, 63, 95, 112, 113, 141, 146, 148

Heaven .28, 38, 40, 49, 52, 53, 91, 92, 113, 123, 124, 125, 126, 150

    banquet of........................ 134

Holy Spirit.. 31, 38, 63, 67, 70, 75, 103, 109, 118, 119, 120, 121, 124, 129, 130, 134, 137, 138, 141, 147, 149, 150, 153, 154, 157

Hope..... 23, 37, 38, 49, 56, 57, 70, 91, 109, 110, 111, 124, 126, 146, 148, 154, 155

Humanity ... 27, 29, 53, 68, 70, 83, 84, 85, 128, 131, 132, 139, 140, 141, 142, 145, 152

    as children of God........... 139

Humility 69, 98

Israel ...41, 42, 100, 102, 119, 120, 127, 128, 140, 155

    Jerusalem 41, 61, 73, 93, 96, 148

    kingdom of 50

    Maccabean Rulers............ 128

    Roman province of Palestine 128

Jesus 28, 30, 53, 55, 57, 62, 63, 67, 72, 80, 81, 84, 85, 93, 94, 95, 96, 97, 98, 100, 101, 102, 103, 109, 111, 112, 113, 118, 119, 120, 121, 123, 124, 125, 126, 127, 128, 129, 138, 139, 140, 141, 145, 146, 148, 151, 152, 154, 155, 156, 157

Jews 50, 62, 73, 102, 122, 137, 140, 144, 153, 156

Judea/Judah.......23, 51, 61, 63, 71, 152, 154, 155

Justice ...24, 26, 37, 38, 41, 70, 85, 103, 108, 118, 119, 121, 128, 138, 139, 140, 141, 142, 153

King, Martin Luther Jr......... 24, 26

King, Martin Luther Jr....... 24, 142

    16th Street Baptist Church 24, 25

Life. 24, 27, 31, 35, 36, 37, 38, 41, 43, 49, 53, 55, 56, 57, 61, 62, 63, 72, 80, 81, 82, 83, 84, 85, 92, 93, 95, 102, 107, 108, 110, 111, 112, 113, 119, 120, 123, 124, 125, 126, 127, 129, 137, 139, 140, 142, 143, 146, 147, 149, 153

    new life 57

Light...... 26, 47, 57, 61, 63, 69, 70, 109, 120, 127, 151, 155, 156, 157

Loneliness 49, 57, 79, 94, 111, 113, 137, 139, 140

Love 31, 35, 37, 38, 41, 48, 49, 53, 57, 69, 70, 73, 74, 75, 80, 81, 82, 83, 85, 92, 94, 95, 96, 97, 107, 108, 109, 110, 112, 113, 119, 121, 128, 130, 139, 141, 142, 144, 145, 146, 149, 150

    agape 139, 140, 142, 145

Luther, Martin 142

Mary Magdalene 55

Merton, Thomas 147, 150

Michelangelo (artist) 147

Names ... 35, 41, 72, 73, 74, 75, 83, 109, 118, 127, 132, 146, 152

Newell, John Philip 150

Pain 36, 57, 80, 81, 82, 94, 107, 111, 112, 113, 126

Persia 155, 156

Physics

    refining metals 51

Power 24, 29, 37, 42, 79, 110, 112, 128, 132, 149

Prayer 23, 28, 41, 42, 43, 70, 74, 89, 96, 98, 103, 113, 138, 139, 140, 142, 146, 148, 149, 150, 157

Princess Bride, The 35, 36

Purity 51, 53, 57

Righteousness ... 24, 26, 37, 42, 52, 118, 120, 124, 137, 138, 139, 141, 153

Rome 50, 55, 79, 96, 98, 100, 125, 128, 137, 156

Sabbath 42, 122

Safety 37, 42, 73, 75, 80, 81, 92, 98, 109, 125

Saints 85, 91, 100, 113, 123, 126

Science

    horticulture 117

    indicator of acidity 53

    mechanical energy 29

    Smartphones 129

Service . 24, 42, 90, 95, 97, 98, 122

Sheep 71, 72, 73, 74, 91, 129

Silver 50, 51, 52, 53, 100, 128

    coins 47, 50, 94

Sin 36, 37, 49, 53, 57, 68, 81, 144, 146, 153

    as dross 52, 53

Slavery .. 47, 48, 96, 100, 101, 102, 124, 125, 145

Spiritual Practice 147, 148

Still, Peter 47

Still, William 47, 49

Testing .. 41, 42, 43, 51, 52, 53, 70, 140

    proof 40, 41, 42, 62

Trickery 68, 149

Trinity 83

Truth 24, 26, 41, 43, 67, 68, 69, 70, 73, 95, 108, 110, 124, 127, 128, 137, 139, 140, 141, 142, 143

Underground Railroad 47

Van Aken, Sam 117

Vengeance ... 26, 35, 36, 37, 69, 73

Vigilance Committee .... *See* Still, William

Violence 23, 24, 25, 26, 55, 72, 74, 80, 92, 108, 109, 110, 128, 137, 138, 141

Violent 42, 109, 124

Vulnerability 80, 81, 84, 141

Wisdom 90, 114, 132

Work 28, 37, 40, 41, 50, 57, 68, 82, 89, 90, 91, 92, 99, 101, 102, 103, 108, 109, 123, 129, 131, 132, 138, 141

Young, Egerton 74

www.ingramcontent.com/pod-product-compliance
Lightning Source LLC
Chambersburg PA
CBHW050202130526
44591CB00034B/1782